Dedicated to all our clients who have taught us that good intentions aren't always good enough for creating successful relations.

Good Intentions Are Not Good Enough

Michelle Garcia Winner
Pamela Crooke

Think Social Publishing, Inc., Santa Clara, California
www.socialthinking.com

Good Intentions Are Not Good Enough
Michelle Garcia Winner and Pamela Crooke

Previously titled *Social Thinking at Work* (2011). New release changes included new title, new cover, and minor content edits and reformatting.

Copyright © 2016 Think Social Publishing, Inc.
All rights reserved except as noted below.

This book may not be copied in its entirety, stored in any retrieval systems, translated, or transferred to an alternative format for any reason without a written license from Think Social Publishing, Inc. (TSP). TSP grants permission to the owner of this product to use and/or distribute select pages of materials from it, "as is" or with owner-created modifications (creating a derivative work), in print or electronic format, only for direct in-classroom/school/home or in-clinic use with your own students/clients/ children, and with the primary stakeholders in that individual's life, which includes the person's parents or caregivers, treatment team members and related service providers.

All other reproduction/copying, adaptation, or sharing/distribution of content in this publication through print or electronic means, requires written licensing from TSP.

All distribution or sharing of materials you create based on this or other TSP works, shared via hard copy or posted electronically on the Internet, or on websites such as YouTube or TeachersPayTeachers.com, whether for free or a fee, is strictly prohibited.

Social Thinking, Superflex, The Unthinkables, The Thinkables, and We Thinkers! GPS are trademarks belonging to TSP.

Visit www.socialthinking.com/ip to find detailed TERMS OF USE information and copyright/trademark FAQs covering using/adapting TSP concepts and materials, speaking on Social Thinking, Superflex or any other parts of our methodology, using the Social Thinking name, etc.

ISBN: 978-1-936943-41-8

Think Social Publishing, Inc.
404 Saratoga Avenue, Suite 200
Santa Clara, CA 95050
Tel: (408) 557-8595
Fax: (408) 557-8594

This book was printed and bound in the United States by Hess Print Solutions. TSP is a sole source provider of Social Thinking products in the U.S.
Books may be ordered online at www.socialthinking.com.

CONTENTS

INTRODUCTION:
The Social Mind: It's Always on the Job, Even When
You're Off the Job vii
    The Social Mind at Work ix
    Multiple Intelligences and Social Learning Challenges xi
    Tools for Social Thinking xii

CHAPTER 1:
Social Thinking: What Is It, and How Is It Different
From Social Skills? 1
    Thinking About Thinking Socially 2
    Emotions and Social Memory 4
    Social Thinking as an Equation 6

CHAPTER 2:
What Plays Into Good Communication Skills? 9
    Strategies for Adult Communication 12

CHAPTER 3:
Emotions: The Uninvited Guest That Keeps Showing Up 29
    Emotional Expression Compression 31
    Exploring the Social-Emotional Chain Effect 33
    Emotional Scale 35
    Problem-Solving Thermometer 41

CHAPTER 4:
Perspective Taking: Are You Thinking What I'm Thinking? 59
    The Seven Core Tenets of Perspective Taking 60

CHAPTER 5:

The Four Steps of Communication:
Talking Isn't the Only Way to Connect ... 71

CHAPTER 6:

The Core of Communication:
What People Mean by What They Say and How They Say It ... 101

    Getting to the Core of Communication ... 106

    Contentious Versus Supportive Relationships ... 112

    Indirect Communication: Reading Between the Lines ... 117

CHAPTER 7:

Fitting In: The Importance of Conformity,
Teamwork and Networking ... 123

CHAPTER 8:

Relating at Work: The Office Hierarchy, Friendship,
Romance and More ... 133

    The Unspoken Codes Around Workplace
    Hierarchy and Culture ... 134

    The Unspoken Codes Around Friendship,
    Flirting and Romance ... 136

    The Unspoken Codes Around Sexual Behavior
    and Bullying ... 140

CHAPTER 9:

Social Technology: How It's Changing the Way We Communicate ... 147

CHAPTER 10:

Social Behavior Maps (SBM) for Adults:
Navigating the Social-Emotional Terrain ... 155

CHAPTER 11:

Strategies: Tips and Pointers ... 169

> "The incredible thing about the human mind is that it didn't come with an instruction book."
> ~ Terry Riley

> "The act of compassion begins with full attention, just as rapport does. You have to really see the person. If you see the person, then naturally, empathy arises. If you tune into the other person, you feel with them."
> ~ Daniel Goleman

Introduction

The Social Mind: It's Always on the Job, Even When You're Off the Job

When people at work say they were, "talking around the water cooler" or "making small talk," what do they really mean? Why is it that someone can come up with a brilliant strategy, but be unable to effectively communicate the idea in a meeting with fellow managers? How is it that a person can be recognized for his productivity on the job, but never is included in the lunchroom social chatter? Where are the social rules of the workplace written, and how come it seems not everyone got the memo?

The "memo," it turns out, is something most people are born with—an intuitive sense that allows them to be naturally aware of social expectations and feeds them the information they need to follow the social code. But not everyone is born with this ability.

Most neurotypical people rely on a built-in "social mining device" (or social radar system) that figures out the "hidden rules" of each social situation—the unwritten code of conduct that everyone is supposed to know and follow—as well as how to assess the various people encountered across a day. They can quickly detect who understands the social code and who doesn't.

If you aren't naturally equipped to absorb or process the necessary information needed to decipher the "social code", it is possible to develop your own social mining device and improve your social ability. It takes time, practice and determination.

One important hidden rule is that social expectations vary by situation, not location. For example, when you come into work in the morning, your colleagues expect you to acknowledge them, if only with a brief look and small smile. However, the next time you see someone during the day, the *situation* has changed—you have already acknowledged the person and do not need to greet him again. How you speak to a coworker is also situationally determined. If you are in a private discussion, you may speak much more casually and openly than if you are presenting the same information in a formal meeting.

Our social radar system gets activated at different times throughout the day, even when we're not planning to speak to anyone. For instance, when we walk into a meeting where we are expected mostly to listen, it's interesting to notice how many thoughts and emotions we have about the people around us. We evaluate whether we "like" the person who is speaking, and we find ourselves aware of those sitting nearby. Even if we won't be talking to most of the people in the room, we'll still have thoughts and related emotions about all of them. And they will have thoughts and related emotions about us.

In fact, we will (or should) adjust our behavior based on what we think people may be thinking about us. For example, if we feel tired and are with other people, we probably won't yawn loudly, close our eyes or put our head down to rest as we might do when we're alone. Why? Because we don't want to call negative attention to ourselves or cause others to have "uncomfortable thoughts" about our behavior or lack of participation. The hidden rules are one way we can figure out what is considered polite and cooperative behavior in a situation. It is a mistake to think there is only one set of "social rules" when at work.

Our social radar system is also in play when we're out in the world, say in a car or on public transit. How we navigate when sharing the road with others and how we maneuver our bodies on a bus or train are guided by what we think people around us are planning next or how our presence is making them feel. So we don't tailgate not only because it is unsafe, but also because we know it probably annoys the driver whom we're following too closely. Even though we don't know this person and will likely never cross his or her path again, we still want to show a sort of respect, or common courtesy, that comes from using our *social thinking*.

We are expected to be constantly aware of who is around us and to anticipate what they plan to do in our shared space. We're also expected to try to figure out *why* people are doing what they are doing, and *how* they may feel when they are doing it. The social mind is on constant alert. While our other systems can often take a rest, the social mind gets almost no time off.

THE SOCIAL MIND AT WORK

Put a dozen coworkers in a room together casually, and notice how almost immediately they break off into smaller groups. What brings them together is not just what is being said, but how others make them feel.

People are more likely to stay if they feel comfortable—if they're included in the conversation (even if the topic is not of particular interest) or are made to feel that others are interested in them. They are less likely to stick around if they feel uncomfortable—if they become overwhelmed by how much another person is talking, for example, or irritated by someone's boasting.

Although most people don't want to acknowledge it, thoughts and emotions—our own and those of others—are some of the most powerful social realities we have to deal with on a daily basis. This is true for both women and men, although they may have different ways of processing and expressing their feelings. One probable reason we don't like to acknowledge our emotions is the high premium placed in our culture on logic and fact. We don't want to think that our feelings or emotional reactions are swaying our responses to the world around us. Nor do we care to acknowledge that how we feel about something or someone is such a powerful determinant in our decision-making. Emotional processing even influences whom we hire and how we work with others. The book *Sway: The Irresistible Pull of Irrational Behavior* (O. Brafman & R. Brafman, 2008) addresses this topic well.

As important as the social mind is, we receive very little instruction about how to operate this complex piece of machinery. As we grow up, our teachers and often our parents give the social mind little attention, and there are even fewer people to coach us in adulthood. We're expected to learn to negotiate, cooperate and respect others intuitively. We are celebrated if our social brain naturally figures out how to work well with people, and we can be shunned, demoted or isolated if our brain does not pick up on the social cues that others grasp easily.

Many people with highly developed minds related to their professions are not nearly as gifted in how they relate to others' minds. Think about the doctor with the poor bedside manners, or the brilliant engineer who can't lead a team of people competently. No matter how intelligent or accomplished these individuals may be in their chosen field of work, if their social mind is not functioning in tandem with their professional mind, this might explain some of the trouble they have operating in the workplace. Or this may be a reason for the lack of promotions they receive compared to other colleagues who may not be as talented in the same field of work.

The social mind has a powerful "social memory" that can hold people accountable for their behavior over time. If we remember that someone criticized an idea without using tact, we are not likely to be a cheerleader for ideas *he* presents. Tit for tat—the social world can be a harsh and unforgiving place. But it can also be warm and encouraging; it has a lot to do with how we play our social cards.

The social world also makes use of "mental manipulation." We occasionally say things we don't truly mean to encourage a person to have a better thought about us or to motivate them to do more for the company. In political campaigns, all candidates make promises they can't or won't uphold. Knowing that, people tend to vote for the candidate they think is telling the fewest lies or offering the ideas they most want to hear. This type of mental play is accepted as a normal human foible. Most any socially neurotypical person will confess to a time he assured a friend she looked good when he didn't really think so, or said that she was doing well when she really wasn't. While as a society we value honesty and integrity, bending the truth to take care of how our words make someone feel or think about us is an accepted form of the social dance.

This book is dedicated to those with social learning challenges. It has been developed from years of working with clients, both children and adults, at our Social Thinking Center in San Jose, California. Those born to a strong academic intelligence but weaker social intelligence can learn more cognitively about the social learning process. For you, the first step in building strengths out of relative learning weaknesses is to understand the concepts outlined in this book. Being able to better understand the expectations of the social mind—even if the concepts are never mastered—has proven to be helpful not only for your own learning, but also for your peace of mind. Our goal is to make information *explicit* by breaking down and defining how the social mind works, and how it is linked to social-emotional and behavioral expectations.

MULTIPLE INTELLIGENCES AND SOCIAL LEARNING CHALLENGES

Many of us grew up with a single idea of intelligence, related to tests we were given in school and how well a teacher or parent thought we were learning academic concepts. Good language skills, a healthy vocabulary and aptitude in one or more subjects are the types of strengths we learned to identify with someone who is "smart."

But the definition of smart should not be based on such limited parameters. Many talented athletes, artists, writers and mathematicians didn't perform well in school; Einstein was one famous example. Looking beyond test scores, it is apparent there are many different kinds of smarts—athletic, artistic, social— more readily gleaned through observation rather than quantified on paper. Howard Gardner, Harvard professor of cognition and author of the seminal book *Frames of Mind* (1993), proposed this concept of multiple intelligences in 1983.

Processing and responding to our own and others' social minds is often referred to as social intelligence or social cognition. Over the years we have met many people who are academically gifted but whose social minds are not fully developed. Many people find it confusing or have trouble accepting that those who are gifted academically can also be weak in their social thinking.

We are good observers of each other's talents and challenges, but we are often the least kind to those who lack social gifts. We do not judge a person who doesn't have natural athletic talent, but we often hear someone with social learning weakness described with isolating adjectives such as *odd, weird, rude* or *arrogant*—because this is how they are perceived.

These individuals face great frustrations. It is not uncommon to find that teachers, counselors, social workers and psychologists are not aware that people can be born with social learning disabilities, and therefore these helping professionals do not create appropriate supports or treatment. Instead they might encourage the person to just "be more social" or "behave better," not realizing that this type of comment can do more harm than good to someone who does not intuitively understand what it all means.

TOOLS FOR SOCIAL THINKING

This book is a primer about the social mind in the workplace but the concepts also apply to home and community settings. It teaches core concepts of how we think about our own and others' thoughts and emotions.

Within these pages you'll explore how the social mind works, how to "hang out" at lunch and better express your thoughts, and how to encourage others to support your personal and professional endeavors. You will also read about things like why work projects can fall flat—not because the ideas aren't good, but because you may not have made the right impression when presenting your concept, or perhaps you failed to support a colleague's idea at another time.

Along the way, you will learn about the dynamic and synergistic factors that help you to determine appropriate social behaviors by understanding the hidden rules of a situation, as well as what you know (or don't know) about the people and their emotions within the situation. The process is complex and it requires social multitasking—social thinking—to encourage people to come back and interact with you again.

Most important, you will explore ideas and specific strategies that you can practice to help develop more "social muscle." The social mind is constantly developing and updating its operating system. You upgrade to *mature* when your social mind works well with others, and to *wise* when you can successfully navigate the nuances and different mind-sets of others, especially people you perceive as being difficult to work with.

After reading this book, you'll never think about making small talk or presenting your ideas in a meeting the same way again. Hopefully, you'll learn how to regularly adjust your thinking and related social behaviors for increasingly successful interactions.

With more social thinking tools at hand, you can make better choices when you're around other people. As many adults who struggle with social issues are painfully aware, it is fine when you choose to be alone, but it is pretty upsetting or disheartening when no one chooses to be with *you*.

POINTS TO CONSIDER

- ❖ We are expected to be constantly aware of who is around us and anticipate what they plan to do in our shared space.

- ❖ As important as the social mind is, we receive very little instruction about how to operate this complex piece of machinery.

> "Life is relationships; the rest is just details."
> ~ Gary Smalley

Chapter 1

Social Thinking
What Is It, and How Is It Different From Social Skills?

Everyone knows someone who can be said to have *good* or *bad* social skills, but few of us have taken much time to think about how social skills develop.

When most people are asked to define what it means to use good social skills, they may say it means being polite or getting along with people. When you dig a little deeper, typically they will say it includes eye contact, reciprocal interaction, respecting other people's space, listening and responding with a related comment, reading nonverbal cues and trying to understand the other speaker's point of view.

While all of these may be true, how about when you're in a situation where there is one person speaking in a room—such as at a conference or in a work meeting—and everyone else is relegated to the role of "listener"? As listeners we are still using good social skills. The fact that we are not talking is what is *expected* in that environment, and being able to sit quietly while looking in the direction of the speaker is the desired, or *good*, social behavior.

How we behave depends not only on the people we are with, but also on the hidden rules embedded in different environments or situations. For example, the types of comments made or jokes told when the CEO is present at a company meeting are very different from the jokes or comments we hear when we go out for a drink with coworkers at the end of the day. The different situations actively feed us information about how to regulate our social behavior.

The use of good social skills, then, is more about *social expectations for particular situations.* This involves being aware of the presence of others and adjusting our behavior based on what people are thinking (or what we want them to think) even in the absence of spoken communication.

Furthermore, having good social skills does not mean always "acting nice." Social skills can be used to discourage interaction, too. A woman holding her purse tightly, avoiding eye contact and walking briskly down the street past a staring man sends a clear nonverbal message to stay away. In the office, when we are busy and don't have time for small talk, we discourage interaction by walking past someone and not stopping to chat.

Combine all this information together, and what emerges is a broader definition of good social skills as *the ability to effectively adapt our social behavior around others according to the situation, what we know about the people in that situation, and what our own needs are.*

THINKING ABOUT THINKING SOCIALLY

When it comes to learning more about social skills, the first thing to appreciate is that they are not skill-based—they are thinking-based. *Social thinking is how we think about our own and others' minds.* Technically referred to as *social cognition*, the term social thinking relates more to what we each do in the personal lab of our own minds, rather than what a team of university researchers might study.

Because our social skills are based largely on this core concept of social thinking, people painted as having good or bad social skills really can be better described as having stronger or weaker related social thinking. To improve our "social performance," or use of social skills, we must hone our ability to figure out what other people are thinking—in other words, how their social minds work. To do this, we have to study how our *own* social mind works.

We all have thoughts about others we share space with. Sharing space means any time we're aware we are in the presence of another person—in a parking garage, in a bathroom or at a board meeting, for example.

Let's imagine that you're entering a large auditorium to listen to a lecture. At the time, it is mostly empty, with only a few people scattered in seats around the room. You now have to choose where to sit. If you sit right next to one of the few persons who is already seated, you will make that person uncomfortable. He'll wonder why you chose to sit right next to him and will try to determine your motive. It's possible he may get up and move to another seat, perhaps mumbling, "Excuse me," or saying nothing at all. If you'd sat a few rows back, he would not have reacted the same way. Why is this true? When the room is filling up, people are expected to take seats at a comfortable distance from each other. It is only when the space gets more crowded and seats are at a premium that new arrivals will start to choose seats that are next to people.

Now, logically, this process makes little sense. Certainly there are more efficient ways to fill up a room—by preassigning seats as is done at concerts or the theater, or by seating people alphabetically (although this really only happens in school). In the situation described above, a more efficient, logical system would be for each person to sit next to someone already seated, and so on, allowing the seats to fill in an orderly fashion. This would solve the problem of vacant seats in the middle of the room left for latecomers, who then have to struggle through the rows of people to sit down. However, social thinking in this situation tells us *it is more important to make decisions based on how we make people feel* rather than on group efficiency.

We have to adapt our social thinking and related social skills to be sensitive to the different people we encounter in a range of situations, regardless of whether we interact with them directly or not.

Pay attention each time you are in the presence of others.

Consider how you adapt your behavior when you are in shared space. For instance, you might take a step forward to allow someone to move around you; otherwise he may think you are rude, or at least not considering his needs.

Our thoughts about each other, even when our interaction is indirect, usually lead to feelings—good or bad.

EMOTIONS AND SOCIAL MEMORY

Like it or not, we are all emotional beings, often navigating our smallest movements in the presence of others simply to guide their emotional response to us. It appears that we are determined to prevent people from having negative feelings about us. Although this phenomenon is something we rarely put into words, our strongest memories of people come from how they tipped our emotional scale, whether positively or negatively. Few of us remember, months or years later, exactly what someone said to make us feel good or bad, but our social memories have strong emotional footprints. The person we remember liking is the one who made us feel good, while the person we think we disliked is whoever made us feel bad—or just uncomfortable.

> In Santa Cruz, California, hundreds of people share the space downtown, mostly passing each other unnoticed. They adapt their social behavior to each others' expectations, doing the social dance with little effort. But there is one person who for many years stood out from the crowd—a local "character." Stories about the Pink Umbrella Man, a middle-aged gentleman believed to have once been an engineer, flew around this college beach town not only because of his eccentricity, but also because of the way he challenged social expectations. Carrying a pink parasol and dressed entirely in pink, including tutu and leotard, he would walk slowly and deliberately down the street, staring ahead, without acknowledging anyone around him. He appeared to lack a purpose or motive; he didn't look

in store windows or interact with people—he didn't even talk to himself. After he walked down one side of the block, he crossed the street and repeated his path in the other direction, day after day. He was the talk of the town. People tried to figure him out, children tried to engage him, many were scared of him. They wondered aloud about his predictable presence and tried to imagine his intentions or figure out the workings of his inner mind. Today if you mention the Umbrella Man, Pink Man or Pink Lady in Santa Cruz or the surrounding towns, virtually everyone knows or remembers him. He tipped their social-emotional memory scales and tattooed himself onto their memories. He is living proof of how social thinking persists, even when we aren't aware of it.

As highly social creatures, we follow a code of social awareness and social adaptability that allows us to live together within society. Although the Pink Umbrella Man seemed harmless, those who don't adapt to our social-emotional expectations can be seen as possible threats. We don't feel we can predict their behavior; therefore we can't decide if they are safe to share space with, or whether we are comfortable being with them.

Social thinking appears to operate in all societies. It is a universal kind of intelligence that is present in all humans, regardless of culture.

No matter where you are in the world, two basic strategies of communication are employed—that you approach a person with whom you intend to communicate, and you look at the person's face to interpret his or her thoughts and emotions. While these strategies are common to all people, the hidden rules that define them are cultural. Put another way, all humans use social thinking to interpret and respond to each other's social signals, but our responses—our social behaviors—are culturally determined.

For instance, how people use eye contact and what they perceive as an appropriate distance for communication are based on culture. In the United States we are expected to look into the face of someone who is speaking to us, but in many Asian cultures children are taught that *not* looking into an adult's eyes is a show of respect. This is not to say that Asian children never look at adults; it is just that during direct communication they are supposed to avert their gaze while an adult addresses them.

These nuances, although incredibly important culturally, come from the same basic social intelligence or social thinking expectations we all share.

On July 16, 2008, a bulletin in the South China Morning Post reported that passengers on a Ningbo bus fled the vehicle when a naked man boarded. The police said he often walked around in the city naked but was not mentally ill.

SOCIAL THINKING AS AN EQUATION

While many people know or can sense when a social interaction or act of communication has resulted in the desired outcome, few of us can explain *how* we relate to each other with our emotions, mind, body, eyes and words to facilitate such an outcome.

No single set of rules governs social behavior across the work or leisure day. The art and skill of the social mind involves figuring out in the moment how to adapt socially to the situation, the person or the culture is—and like any other aspect of our minds, it can develop and change with the proper tools to explore it.

Social thinking drives our social behavior and responses. Thinking socially can help us change our behavior, and by changing our behavior we are directly affecting how we are being perceived socially. While we are doing this, we are simultaneously interpreting other people's social behavior to try and figure out what *they* are thinking!

Considering and responding to so many often-simultaneous factors is quite a complex process—a *socially algebraic equation*. Any time a part of the equation changes, so does the behavior, the interpretation of the behavior and the response to the behavior. If two colleagues are talking and a third person enters the group, how they talk to each other and what they talk about may change noticeably, and sometimes significantly, now that the equation has changed.

Social behavior is relatively easy to detect when it is not being used well. However, it is far more complicated to understand how we decide *what* to do and *when* we should do it. Remarkably, it is a process that most of us manage well at least some of the time. But it is also something every one of us messes up, and this happens more often than any of us would like to admit.

To complicate things further, we are not always good judges of our own social behavior. We know how we feel about other people, but not necessarily how they feel about us. We interpret their social skills, and they interpret ours. How we do this is based on many variables, including emotions, points of view, life experiences, the particular situation, what we know about the people in that situation, tone of voice, body language, what we say and what we don't say. Most of us, including even those people whom others see as socially gifted, have insecurities about our social skills. In fact, anyone who announces "I have really good social skills" usually does not!

We will delve into all of these ideas in the coming chapters, starting by taking a closer look at what makes good communication skills. By attempting to make the abstract concrete, you can to become a better observer, and then a participant, in your own constantly changing social world.

POINTS TO CONSIDER

❖ The art and skill of the social mind involves figuring out how to adapt socially in the moment.

❖ Social thinking appears to operate in all societies. It is a universal kind of intelligence that is present in all humans, regardless of culture.

❖ Our strongest memories of people come from how they tipped our emotional scale, whether positively or negatively.

www.dilbert.com, ©1991 United Feature Syndicate, Inc.

> "Communication works for those who work at it."
> ~ John Powell

> "The most important thing in communication
> is to hear what isn't being said."
> ~ Peter Drucker

Chapter 2

What Plays Into Good Communication Skills?

The first step in understanding social thinking is recognizing that we all have thoughts about the people around us all of the time. We use social thinking when we're talking with someone, when we're observing others and even when we're not interacting directly. If you see a person coming toward you down a narrow hallway and you move to the side, you are using social thinking in that small moment, even if neither of you says a word.

We also have thoughts about interactions that happened long after the people are in our presence. As you review an encounter that may not have been as satisfying as you'd hoped, it is often helpful to call or e-mail to clarify your intentions and patch up any misunderstanding. Or you may realize that you just didn't pay enough attention to someone (you failed to communicate), and you might contact her to say you didn't mean to brush her off or act as if you were upset; you might say that you were just distracted by other thoughts or had something on your mind.

Kyle was walking up the stairs in his office building when a coworker passed him and said, "Hi," but he did not hear her. As they continued in opposite directions, the woman said, "Hi" again, but in a loud voice. Kyle greeted her in return, and was surprised when the woman called his office shortly after to ask why he seemed angry with her. He said he was not angry, but she would not accept his answer and insisted he tell her the truth. He said he did not feel comfortable talking to her any longer and hung up the phone. He called a coworker to complain about the incident, but the woman had beaten him to it, saying that Kyle was acting angry and refusing to talk about it. When Kyle explained that he simply did not hear her first greeting, the coworker said it could not have been such a simple misunderstanding, and there must have been something that Kyle did. Now Kyle really was angry! How could he be so misinterpreted? His intentions were good!

The intricate balance of making sure other people feel OK while sharing what is on our own minds is time-consuming, and it is at the heart of successful or failed work relationships. Social interactions take more work than we like to admit!

The reality is that we *all* care what others think about us, although we aren't always comfortable acknowledging it. Even people who insist they don't care probably still feel bothered when someone doesn't like them or finds their ideas unappealing.

Social psychology, or being aware of other people's social thoughts, is a requirement of functioning in a society regardless of culture. The following is a list of some social needs and requirements that we all share—being that we are individuals who function as members of a society.

- We all want others to have reasonable or good thoughts about us as often as possible.
- We all worry that others don't like us.
- We all have to focus on trying to make those around us feel OK, even when we don't plan to interact.
- We all have to be aware that people try and read our intentions, but we cannot be sure they are reading them ac-

curately. We need to monitor how others are thinking to ensure we are having reasonable reciprocal social thoughts about each other.

- We all have to monitor and possibly adjust our behavior to help people read our intentions the way we want them to be read. So, for example, we may have to look attentive when we're feeling bored, act as if we are interested in someone's idea so he or she will consider our idea, or simply say "Hi" in a friendly voice, even when the person is irritating us!

On the flip side, there are times when we want to distance ourselves from certain people or indicate that we are not available to communicate. So what do we do when we don't want to interact? We modify our social behavior to send the desired message—by looking down at our work when someone walks by, glancing at our watch when a colleague is talking to us, or simply saying in a friendly voice, "I'm sorry I can't talk right now. I have a lot to get done today. Can we talk later?"

We often use nonverbal communication to signal unavailability in different types of situations, say, for instance, when someone is walking down the street and sees someone who looks suspicious to them. Notice how the person walks more quickly, holds their bags tighter and avoids looking directly at the suspicious person.

Any time we monitor and adjust our social behaviors (posture, tone of voice, gestures, gaze, walking speed, physical proximity) to control the way we interact, so long as we don't cause the other person to feel angry, we are likely using good social thinking and related social skills. When this is done well, we can get our needs met without upsetting others.

It is important to recognize that employing good social thinking and related social skills does not mean you always have to try to please people or make them happy. It means that you are *strategic* in deciding who you want to relate to and how you want them to think about you, both in the short and long term.

STRATEGIES FOR ADULT SOCIAL COMMUNICATION

Social thinking is the mindset we use to consider the people we share space with, whether for a moment, a day, a month or longer. *Social skills* are the social behaviors we use to demonstrate our related social thinking.

Social skills are not static or fixed, however, and how we use our skills varies depending on whom we're talking to, the setting and the situation.

People often talk about "social rules" (also known as "hidden rules"), which are more guideposts than edicts. By the time we are adults, our social behavior plays out with nuance and some sophistication. For instance, rather than always following the simple rule to use eye contact to show we are listening, as adults we need to recognize that there are different ways to use our eyes, depending on the situation. At a small meeting, full-on, intense staring at the speaker can be overwhelming and make the person uncomfortable. A better use of eye contact would be to keep our eyes on the speaker generally, while also looking around a bit and occasionally shifting our glance to follow what the speaker is saying.

The difference is in the subtle use of the skill. The way we use a particular social skill can determine how comfortable people feel with us or whether they want to include us in their social network.

Next time you're in a meeting, at a café or somewhere out in the world, observe groups of folks around you. Notice how much you can learn about relationships from the little ways people treat each other. A slight turn of the shoulder may mean "I don't want to talk to you anymore." Two people who linger, looking into each other's eyes, may be flirting or already a couple.

A key to understanding why people seem to think so much about each other is to realize that many of us are born with a social curiosity. We wonder about all different aspects of other people's lives. From a social evolutionary point of view, this type of thinking keeps us alert to who is around us and what their motives are; in that way it provides a degree of personal security. From a social relationship point of view, our curiosity keeps us trying to connect with what we share in common and find interesting about each other.

However, many adults with social learning challenges are born with weak social curiosity; they don't often wonder what people are thinking, feeling or doing in their presence. Instead, they are under the incorrect impression that since *they* know their own intentions are good, everyone else simply must know it, too. When they are misunderstood or perceived as unfriendly, they feel terrible and often become depressed or anxious.

The information in the sections below provides you with more concrete ways to look at all of this abstract material, and it may help you understand why the nuances of communication can have such a profound effect on how other people evaluate and consider us.

What are the Hidden Rules or Expectations in the Situation?

Just like a good story, communication starts by establishing the context, setting or situation. What is appropriate to say or do in one situation may not be appropriate for another. Understanding the situation helps you to figure out the hidden rules or expectations. The reason they are described as hidden is that we rarely discuss or acknowledge them; they are just a given. And of course the reason they are called expectations is because everyone is expected to know them.

The place or setting itself does not always define the rules of use; instead, you have to look at the particular situation to establish what the social expectations might be.

In our office, the space off the kitchen is known as the break room. However, people also have meetings in the break room throughout the day—except first thing in the morning, when everyone is putting their lunches or snacks in the kitchen, and during lunchtime, when people come together to eat. No signs are posted on the door to define what is happening in the break room at any given time; each person is expected to enter the space as an observer, picking up on the nonverbal or verbal cues to determine how the space should be shared. The social behavior that is expected and tolerated in the break room varies considerably based on the situation, and not on the space itself.

In essence, then, to use social thinking and related skills well, we have to be constant social observers and problem-solvers. We must try to determine what is going on in a situation and what our role is (if any) to be effective. For instance, many times during the workday you probably pass by people who are in conversation. Usually the way to share the space is simply to keep moving through it, without saying anything or acknowledging the people in the space. But at times it may be appropriate to stop and join in the conversation.

So how do you determine when you should talk or not, stay and listen or not, or pretend you haven't heard something you've heard? You evaluate the situation and what you know about the people in it.

An example of situational expectations is played out in the following scenario, in which a coworker is packing up his belongings to leave at the end of a long day and you want to speak to him about a project.

Expected Behavior	Unexpected Behavior
Let your coworker know you want to talk to him in the morning about an idea for the project.	Tell your coworker you want to meet with him right then about an idea you are considering.
Ask your coworker if he has any evening plans (simply to show you are interested in him).	Tell your coworker at length what your after-work plans are but fail to ask about his plans.
Tell your coworker to have a good evening.	Don't acknowledge your co-worker at all as he leaves the office; just watch him leave.

An expected behavior keeps people feeling calm or causes them to have good thoughts about the person performing the behavior. An unexpected behavior makes others have weird or uncomfortable thoughts about the person which leads to feeling awkward, frustrated or any range of emotions.

To explore expected and unexpected behaviors in different situations, make a list of the different possible behaviors, verbal and nonverbal (such as tone of voice, gestures, eye contact or facial expressions) and whether these are *expected* or *unexpected* in that situation.

Who is Present, and What Do I Know About Them?

The more we consider what we know about people's personalities and their roles at work, the more that information can determine how, when or whether we should communicate with them.

Familiarity creates its own set of expectations. For example, if you've become pretty comfortable with someone but don't acknowledge her when she comes into the office, it may make her wonder if something is wrong (remember Kyle?). Conversely, if you don't know a coworker and have not spoken to him before, other than saying "Hi," yet you act very friendly and ask what he did last night, it can also lead to an uncomfortable thought.

Here's another scenario: You attend an office party where the president of your company is present. You've never spoken to her before, but she's friendly and supportive at the party and you enjoy a casual discussion with her. The next day at the office, she appears busy and professional. Even though you had a nice conversation with her yesterday, it doesn't mean you can socialize with her today, because things should be back to business as usual.

Friendly can mean different things, too. Sometimes it can be about engaging in a lively conversation, while other times it means simply a small, quick smile commonly used to acknowledge another person in passing. The better we learn to read or figure out people's emotions, the quicker we can determine when they need personal space, or when they could use some extra support or just our presence. Keep in mind that certain situations, such as a meeting, are not right for addressing personal issues, even if we know someone is upset.

As you come into an office, start by observing and trying to identify the basic social expectations of the work environment. Then you can start to figure out the people—what you know about them, and what you don't know about them.

What are the Time Demands in the Situation?
Much of work is defined by time. We start and end at specific times, and throughout the day our workflow is segmented by time. Meetings usually are set for specific times, and often we define times for certain tasks. Many of us use the clock to set goals—"I want to get this done by 10 a.m.," for example.

It is important to remember that communication itself takes time. As we carve out time to communicate with others, we have to keep in mind we are taking *their* time. A major complaint of employees is when a coworker chats too much or doesn't get to the point fast enough. Few of us have patience for the person who takes time away from the internal schedule that drives us across a workday.

> Zac felt it was critical to share his ideas with others—all of his ideas, and in great detail. We noticed when he came to our office that it was difficult to get him to stop talking and engage on other topics. We asked how much he had talked to his coworkers at a previous job, and he said, "It wasn't a problem. If I spent a couple of hours talking to a person, it worked out fine. Since I'm not married and I don't have kids, I could stay late to get all my work done."

A point Zac missed was that while his lengthy conversations didn't pose a problem for *him*, they may have been excruciating for his coworkers. Some people will go to great lengths to avoid a coworker they think will take up their time.

When communicating with one another, we should pay attention to how our coworkers are sensitive to time. We will often hear, "I need about ten minutes to talk to you about the project. Is this a good time?" or "Hey, can I get back to you in a few minutes? I really need to finish up what I was doing here," or "Can you make it quick?" or "I can't talk right now, I have too much on my plate. I'll call you later." If you start hearing these kinds of statements from your coworkers frequently, it may mean you aren't being aware of how much time you are taking from them. Listen carefully to the message being conveyed and be respectful of it.

Something that's essential to keep in mind, is that people almost never directly tell you what they're thinking or how they want you to act (although they may allude to it). Understanding this is a key to interpreting social information and creating appropriate social responses.

> Zac constantly heard the kinds of comments noted above that signaled he was not being aware of other people's time. Coworkers said they would "get back" to him, but they never did. Zac got angry and felt they were leaving him out. Eventually, he was fired. Zac was a skilled worker, but he didn't adapt socially in the workplace, and he talked so much that people complained and felt they couldn't work with him.

How is My Behavior Expected to Change with Age?

We all notice that children move through a range of social behaviors as they grow, but as adults many of us aren't aware that we also continue to make these kinds of changes throughout our lives.

Language and nonverbal mannerisms are expected to evolve to correspond with our chronological age. These shifts occur below the level of detection, but if you stand back and observe a fifty-year-old lawyer talking to a twenty-six-year-old lawyer, you will notice significant differences in their social behavior. The twenty-six-year-old lawyer will use one set of social skills when meeting with the older lawyers in his firm and another when hanging out with similar-age peers at lunch.

The fact that we are *all* learning and making adjustments in our social thinking and related social skills as we age should be encouraging. The social brain is alive and learning at all ages. In fact, once someone has mastered social thinking, we consider them to be wise—and wisdom is a characteristic we usually attribute to people in their seventies and eighties.

> The CEO of a company asked a twenty-three-year-old new hire how everything was going. She said she was doing "really well" with the job and "understood everything." Knowing how much people have to learn in a work environment, the CEO responded, "Well, that could be a problem if you know everything, because the rest of us are still trying to figure it all out!" The new hire quickly retracted her words. "I didn't really mean that," she said. "I'm just grateful for all the help I'm getting."

Awareness of social expectations based on age is important. It is expected that some young new hires may come to the job overconfident, maybe a bit cocky, certain they know more than they really do. But they are not yet savvy about how the information they learned in school is put to work in the *real world*. A fifty-year-old may write off the arrogant behavior of a twenty-year-old as "youthful thinking," but is not as quick to excuse the same behavior from a forty-five-year-old. The older worker understands through experience that no one really knows it all—or is expected to!

> We recently assessed a fifty-two-year-old who had returned to school to get her PhD. She had a history of negative social encounters in the work environment and now in the academic setting. When she got upset with people, she often ended up telling them they didn't understand her, and then she'd begin to cry and sometimes yell. This behavior was considered very problematic in

someone her age, although it may have been more excusable if it happened (very infrequently) with a young employee.

Are There Different Ways to Give Compliments?

Being emotional animals, we all enjoy it when people show they approve of our behavior and ideas.

As children we are taught to give compliments. Teachers might encourage students to tell a classmate, "I like your drawings," or "You are really good at that." As we mature, our compliments become far more nuanced. While it is always nice to verbally acknowledge a job well done, there are many opportunities to give indirect compliments as well. In fact, the greatest indirect compliment we can give someone is by simply paying attention and showing interest in his ideas or thoughts.

There are several ways to do this. Here are a few ideas:

- Show interest by listening to someone's idea and asking questions to elicit information (but not for the purpose of collecting this information to present your point of view).

- Encourage a coworker to share ideas. For example, "I read your notes on the project. Can you tell me more about your thinking?" Or you can indicate you want help in making a decision: For example, "Where should we go for lunch—what's your favorite place?"

- Invite a colleague to join you for lunch or a walk.

- Ask about things you remember that a coworker enjoys (family, hobbies). For example, "How's your daughter doing at college?"

- Choose a person to work on your team.

However, when showing interest in another person, there is a fine line between underplaying it and overplaying it. If you give someone a compliment, direct or indirect, but then the rest of the week don't show any personal interest, that person may not believe you really meant what you said. On the other hand, being *too* attentive is equally problematic.

Observe others in the work environment and think about the differences in how people relate to each other when they are close friends, versus when they are just workmates, versus when they barely know each other. This will establish a basis for understanding how the people in your workplace relate to each other. The goal is to relate in a friendly but unobtrusive and professional manner.

How to Apologize

Just as we teach children how to give compliments, we also teach them how to apologize. However, few of us still use the same apology strategies as when we were five years old. Simply stating we are sorry is not enough and does not convince people we actually *feel* sorry. As adults, demonstrating remorse is most important.

At times we need to apologize even if we don't necessarily feel we did anything wrong. For example, if someone interpreted that you were angry by the way you communicated, but you feel you were not acting angry, rather than argue you would say, "I'm sorry I made you feel that way." This doesn't mean you are saying you are wrong; you are simply acknowledging that the other person had negative feelings and that it wasn't your intention for that to happen. Apologizing shows people you are sensitive to their emotions.

In many instances we may start our apology with words, but we must follow up with more intentional ways of indicating regret to *show* the person we are sorry. Some of those ways may be

- Going beyond saying "sorry" to admitting you were wrong. On an airplane one flight attendant who had left some important material out on the counter said to another, "I should have put it back. My mistake, sorry!" They both smiled at each other and moved on.

- Avoiding making the same mistake in the future. Our apologies or apologetic behavior may be accepted, but if you make the same or a similar mistake over and over again, then you are failing to monitor how your behavior is affecting others and you will be perceived as unremorseful.

- Apologizing for how you made the other person feel, regardless of whether you felt he misunderstood your intentions!

As kids, we were taught to apologize when we got into a conflict. While this continues to be a good rule of thumb, it is far better to learn to avoid conflict by anticipating other people's thoughts and feelings and then creating a response that keeps us emotionally connected and others calm.

How Do I Ask for Help?

Most people like to be asked to give help every once in a while. It's another way of giving a compliment—by indicating that the person knows something you may not, or that you value his or her input in thinking through a problem.

Many persons who have social learning challenges don't understand the value of asking others for help. They may like to give help, but they don't see how *not* asking for help can be perceived negatively.

When we ask for help, it does not necessarily mean we need HELP! It simply means we would like someone to provide a different point of view and help to problem-solve something we are stuck on. Asking for help also can simply mean seeking clarification on a work-related question or just asking for an opinion on our own ideas.

Asking for help shows your willingness to let other people influence your thinking. Rather than start with something important, instead ask for help with a small matter. In this way, you build social relationships and learn to trust that people can help make your day easier.

As with any social skill, practice is what leads to improvement.

Steven was a talented architect who was told he needed to improve his teamwork skills. He acknowledged that he rarely asked for help at work, and he agreed to practice. Coincidentally, he had just been in a bicycling accident and had broken his collarbone. When we asked if he had anything he might need help with at work, Steven said he had to set up a new computer and had planned on doing it himself, even though one of his arms was fully splinted. For the past year, Steven had been in an office with one other person but had never spoken to him. We encouraged Steven to consider how his coworker might think of him if he walked by and saw Steven struggling with a computer when he could have asked for help. It did not come naturally to Steven, but it was not beyond him to learn to ask for help, especially when he was told that we all have thoughts about each other, even when we aren't interacting directly. Steven became motivated to work to change those thoughts by changing his behavior, and eventually he was able to ask his coworker to help him.

Whom do we ask for help? As young students we're taught to go to the teacher, but by middle school most students ask their peers for help. In high school, college, in the workplace or community, we are almost completely peer-dependent in getting help.

At work, the first people to turn to are the peers with whom you work most directly. If they aren't sure of the answer, or the question or problem requires more advanced knowledge than they can provide, you would then seek out your project or team manager—quietly and discreetly, away from the keen eyes and ears of the colleagues you just asked for help.

For example, if you ask Maddie for help but aren't sure she has given the information you need, and you walk a couple of feet over and ask Peter the same question, Maddie will be offended. She will interpret your behavior—going to Peter with the same question—as not appreciating her attempt to help you. But if you seek out Peter when Maddie isn't around, you are using tact, or skill, in dealing with sensitive situations. You get the information you need while being emotionally sensitive to how the people around you are feeling.

As important as it is to ask for help, doing so constantly (unless you are newly hired) or persistently seeking assistance from someone too high up in the company hierarchy can make you appear to be socially unaware and insensitive to the work culture. As with all social communication, asking for help requires social thinking and related skills to understand the hidden rules.

If You Get Started on the Wrong Foot, How Do You Change Your Image?

People are pretty quick to size someone up, form an initial impression, learn more about the person, create some social memories and then adhere their thinking to what they believe they know about that person—whether right or wrong.

The way others perceive us can feel completely counter to who we think we really are and make us feel misunderstood. Yet once people have pegged someone and created social memories, they do not easily let go of those memories. To change how others think about us and remember us, we must alter our social behavior to alter the social perception.

Trying to tweak someone's perception is no simple task and cannot be hastened by an apology or explanation. Telling someone we're going to be a "better listener" or "be less argumentative" is called "talking the talk." If we want people to shift their overall impression of us, we also have to *be* better listeners and *be* less argumentative. We have to "walk the walk"—not just for a day, but consistently, every day.

The reality is that there will be people who don't like us no matter how well we use our social thinking, and people we don't like in return. Then we have reason to avoid each other. We don't necessarily need to try and change every negative perception someone might have of us.

There are times, however, when we have to relate positively to someone we don't particularly like, and who we know doesn't care for us either. In this situation, we do the "social fake" and our social behavior is more complimentary, even if we don't think the person is deserving of our display of friendliness and tolerance.

In the work environment, the goal is to get along with coworkers, regardless of how we personally feel about them. It is fair to say this is a significant challenge for virtually everyone at some point. Demonstrating social maturity means adapting our behavior to keep the work environment constructive rather than destructive, allowing each person to do the job he or she is being paid to do, and not getting sidetracked by personal on-the-job conflicts.

Why Are Greetings Not as Benign as They Appear?

Greetings, as goofy as it sounds, are the lubricant in the social operating system. They show people you are thinking about and acknowledging them.

If you are going to choose someone to talk to during the day, will it be the person who acknowledges you in the hall by saying "hi," or the person who walks right by as if you aren't there?

Saying "hi" requires more than a verbalization. Essential in all greetings is acknowledging the person with your eyes. The act of greeting people with "hi" or "bye" connects your eyes with your words, smile or nod. You look toward the person you want to greet, and as you walk past and he or she looks your way, you have some choices:

- You can say, "Hi" or "Hey" or "Good morning."
- You can say, "How are you?"
- You can smile and not say anything.
- You can say, "Hi" and give a small wave, raising your hand slightly to acknowledge the person.
- You can look at the person and nod with your chin, lifting it slightly and then quickly lowering it again, coupled with a small smile.

If you are leaving for the day, the greeting also begins with eye contact but then is followed by:

- "Have a good night."
- "Bye."
- "See you tomorrow."
- "Take it easy."
- The small hand wave (this can be included but is optional).
- Looking at the person with a small smile and slightly lifting your chin and then quickly lowering it again.

But don't start practicing greetings by saying "Hi" to everyone you see at work; that would be overdoing it. Observe people as they pass by and identify just one or two you would feel comfortable greeting. These are likely people with whom you have worked with successfully in the past and want to continue developing your working relationship. Or it might be a person you pass frequently who acknowledges you with a small greeting or head nod.

Consider your own response patterns. If you recognize that you would benefit from using more positive behaviors—such as asking for help, giving indirect compliments or saying "Hi"—begin by setting manageable goals for yourself.

If you want to practice being friendly in the work setting, you will want to increase the number of times you greet people at the start of the workday. The first week, don't change your behavior at all; instead just observe which people you'd like to say "Hi" to. The next week begin by looking toward the one or two on your mental list and saying "Hi" or acknowledging them nonverbally. If you start with very high goals ("Today I will be friendly and say 'Hi' to everyone at work!"), you will quickly wear yourself out and feel like you failed at the task. Even if you succeed in greeting everyone at work, this can create *weird thoughts* in others, because their social memory is that you have never done this before and therefore your behavior is unexpected and hard to interpret.

Social behaviors need to change subtly to be effective.

What seems like such a simple thing isn't that simple to people who weren't born able to figure it out intuitively. Understandably, this type of skill, which comes so easily to neurotypical people, can feel overwhelming and complicated to those who have not practiced it all of their lives.

No special training is needed to be a judge of someone else's social behavior, and coworkers can be astute diagnosticians when it comes to identifying someone who is not acting socially "appropriate." They can be harsh judges of those folks who are more clumsy in their navigation of social waters. This can be extremely frustrating for those of us who are technically proficient at the job but not well liked or well respected because of weaknesses in relating socially.

It is an ongoing challenge to think about how others perceive us, and then target specific ways to modify our social skills so we are perceived more positively. This type of work is what we all do every single day. If you happen to work with people who are trying to improve their social functioning, give them credit. It is not an easy thing to do! And if you are trying to improve your own social functioning, be patient with your coworkers. It may take time for them to adapt to the changes you are making.

This chapter, with its discussion of some of the complex variables we use to relate to each other, is a good place to begin exploring your social behavior and thinking about how others may be interpreting and responding to it.

Good Intentions Are Not Good Enough

POINTS TO CONSIDER

❖ If you are going to choose someone to talk to during the day, will it be the person who acknowledges you in the hall by saying "Hi" or the person who walks right by as if you aren't there?

❖ In the work environment, the goal is to get along with co-workers, regardless of how we personally feel about them.

❖ To use social thinking and related skills well, we have to be constant social observers and problem-solvers.

❖ To change how others think about us and remember us, we must alter our social behavior to alter the social perception.

❖ As we carve out time to communicate with others, we have to keep in mind we are taking their time.

www.dilbert.com, ©2004 Scott Adams, Inc.

"[I]t is very hard to say the exact truth, even about your own immediate feelings — much harder than to say something fine about them which is not the exact truth."

~ George Eliot

"You cannot make yourself feel something you do not feel, but you can make yourself do right in spite of your feelings."

~ Pearl S. Buck

Chapter 3

Emotions
The Uninvited Guest That Keeps Showing Up

Next we'll look at the "e-word." Emotions are rulers of our social world, whether we want to empower them or not. Even without our full awareness, emotions serve as an omnipresent decision-maker in our daily social interactions.

Caleb, a gifted child with an IQ of 150 who enjoyed physics and learning about black holes, refused to acknowledge his own emotions. When encouraged to recognize his feelings of sadness and happiness, he insisted angrily, "I don't have emotions!"

***

Chithra, a forty-year-old graduate student, is at risk of getting expelled from her university program if she shows another fit of rage while on campus. Her professor acknowledges that she is academically brilliant.

We've all experienced times when we wished we could just turn our thoughts off, whether we're sleeping, daydreaming or fully alert. We humans are thinkers day and night. Most of our thoughts generate feelings, and our feelings nearly always produce emotional responses. The responses can range from something as simple as a feeling of contentment to something more complex and upsetting like stress, irritation or anger.

Emotions can lead us into action. It even can be said that our emotions *drive* us into action. We may lash out at someone when we're feeling down, and be more playful when we're happy, all without much forethought or contemplation.

In fact, emotions are considered "contagious". Research on this idea and related theories shows that we respond to situations based on how people around us seem to feel. If someone is upset, we are more apt to be upset, too, and if people are upbeat or outgoing, we are more likely to have positive interactions.

As powerful as emotions are in our lives and as to how we function, they are just as elusive to study and quantify. In part, this is because most of us aren't all that forthcoming when it comes to discussing our emotions. It's not uncommon to even tell little lies about how we feel or how others made us feel.

Many who pride themselves on their intellect and logic will dismiss or deny their emotions altogether. In fact, the mere discussion of emotions can generate a kind of fear response. But our emotions are a shadow to our being, and they insist on our attention even if we try to bury or ignore them.

As much as some may admire the sentient android Data on *Star Trek* for being smart but emotionally unaffected by what goes on around him, an employee with this type of flat, emotionless personality is often perceived as a weak team player and is not typically considered gifted in the workplace. This is the case no matter how well he or she does the job or how intellectually brilliant he or she is. Logic and emotions can and do coexist, as the following example shows.

Tom, an engineer in his forties, was a husband and father who made decisions for his family based purely on logic, never factoring in emotions—either his own or his wife's. Her negative reactions confused Tom, given what he perceived to be his ironclad decision-making skills. His wife had him seek counsel to come to terms with his emotions. He learned that emotions are omnipresent, and his own fluctuated throughout the day between mild irritation and mild satisfaction, occasionally moving into anger or joy. Tom began to chart his emotions in fifteen-minute increments and was fascinated to observe the way his feelings drove how he responded to situations. He was not "fine" all day, as he originally thought. This information also helped him to be aware that others, including his family and his coworkers, had similar emotions and that he needed to pay attention and be responsive to them.

EMOTIONAL EXPRESSION COMPRESSION

Although we have different levels of emotions across the day, we *act* as if we are fairly well put together: patient, attentive, focused. In other words, we are expected to compress the expression of our emotional responses. This is something most of us naturally figure out how to do as we grow up. It is part of what we refer to as "maturing."

However, many adults struggle to master the concept of emotional regulation—meaning small things still bother them and are expressed largely. If they are upset, the whole office knows about it. Even though this may be an honest response, the problem is that it makes others uneasy. We usually seek to be in the company of people who are emotionally stable. We feel safer with people who we don't feel are going to explode or get upset when things don't go exactly right.

How we express and compress our emotions (verbally and nonverbally) changes with age. By age fourteen, teenagers, when they are with their friends, show relatively little emotion on their faces, even when they are feeling relatively large emotions internally. They may act as if something is *no big deal*, when in fact they are feeling incredibly sad or frustrated.

Typically, as we mature, we understand better how to control the *size* of our emotional response, since we can't entirely control the emotions themselves. By the time we are adults in the workforce, we are expected to express our emotions with much subtlety and refinement. We don't walk around work looking either glum or excited. Regardless of the emotions we experience internally, we appear to others to be relatively even and calm.

Interestingly, many of the same adults we have worked with who have not learned to compress their emotional responses also often seem unaware that people can be upset but not react by showing strong negative emotions. By the time we are teenagers, most of us are able to recognize in context when someone is upset just by noticing he isn't smiling in our presence, or he is moving his brow slightly to show discontent.

Countless numbers of our clients who are unable to pick up on these kinds of facial or verbal clues will complain that no one ever says or shows when they are upset. They easily miss the subtle social behaviors used to convey emotions. They fail to read the cues and mistakenly believe their coworkers are completely satisfied with them. Imagine their surprise when they are told in a job review that their coworkers have been dissatisfied with how they are relating at work. Our clients leave these meetings completely mystified, unclear where they have misstepped. Furthermore, if they are doing the job they were hired to do, they can't understand why anyone even *cares* how they feel, or why emotions are important in the first place.

The very fact they are upset about how others feel simply demonstrates how emotional they are *themselves*!

An important word about our bodies and minds

While this book is focused on cognitive strategies we use to interpret the social emotional world around us and our related responses, our minds don't work efficiently if our bodies are not helping us to keep calm. As adults we are expected to have subtle strategies we can call on to help us stay relaxed and calm ourselves when we start to feel overwhelmed. Taking some deep breaths, is one of those many strategies. As we talk about emotions and stress, consider how good you are at noticing when your body feels relaxed or is highly stressed. Some of us need to begin emotional management by first recognizing our physiological signs of stress (for example, shoulders tense, feelings of discomfort in the body). As adults many of us seek more sophisticated physical methods for stress reduction, yoga being one of many choices. The body and mind are connected to help us have access to thinking through the social thinking process; we often need to have our bodies helping us to establish the calm that helps us to think more clearly.

Some of our clients with social thinking challenges also have a life long history of what is referred as *sensory regulation problems*. This means they may be hypersensitive or hyposensitive to changes in the environment (for example, light, sound, touch) making it difficult for their body to adapt in ways that are helpful to establish an inner calm. Occupational therapists are part of a field of professionals that has emerged in the last 20 years to help clients learn strategies to deal more effectively with their sensory imbalances or lack of sensory integration, helping them facilitate inner focus and calm, allowing their ideas and thoughts to flow with fewer interruptions. If you feel your body works against your mind in the way it processes and responds to sensory input in different situations, contact an occupational therapist in your community who specializes in sensory integration.

EXPLORING THE SOCIAL-EMOTIONAL CHAIN EFFECT

The dynamic connection between our own emotions and the emotions of others can be thought of as a *chain effect* that triggers positive and negative responses, influencing the way we feel about each other. We will focus on the essential utility of emotions and look at their role as the basis of our social processing and decision-making.

The Social-Emotional Chain Effect is a logical, theoretical way of understanding the pieces of the social puzzle and how we universally interpret and respond to emotions—our own and those of others. Interactions at work and with friends require us to sort all of this out. You may find it easier to start by recognizing your feelings as they relate to friendships than to examine how your emotions fit into the ties you form at work.

The nine facets described below do not necessarily happen in sequence, but instead play off one another. They coexist within a dynamic, synergistic system that is in operation both inside and outside of work. In this system, perceptions, thoughts and feelings weave into the greater emotional tangle of human relationships.

THE SOCIAL-EMOTIONAL CHAIN EFFECT

1. **We recognize our own emotional responses/feelings.** Although we are rarely encouraged to talk about our feelings in the work setting, we are still expected to recognize them and keep them under control. In other words, we maintain an air of emotional stability, even when we don't truly feel all that stable, and at the same time we are sensitive to our emotions and the emotions of others.

    Emotions fluctuate on a regular but not always predictable basis. For example, on a day that we anticipated eagerly, we may wake up cranky or on the "wrong side of the bed" and not respond to others as positively as we'd hoped.

    When a coworker greets us in the morning by asking, "How are you?" we're expected to say "Fine" or "OK." Even if we come to work in a bad mood after a huge argument at home with our teenager, we are still expected to answer, "Fine" when asked, and then ask our coworker the same question in return, and expect a response in kind.

    With close friends we can be more forthright and say how we are really feeling, as long as we do it at the right time and in the right place.

    Take a look at the accompanying scale of emotional

responses. Across the middle is a line that says "Fine or OK." It's there for the many people who insist they are *always* fine, even if their tone of voice or general disposition appear to betray their words. I have worked with adults who one day say in a friendly voice, "I'm fine!" and on another day say in a labored, flat tone, "I'm fine." Even though they insist they feel the same way both days, I interpret their responses differently because of *how* they answer the question.

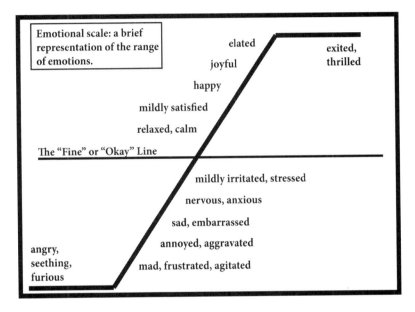

The scale represents the range of emotions we feel and respond to over a day, a week, a year—a lifetime. Below the "OK" line are shades of negative emotions. While the order may vary from person to person, the idea is to move from mild to more serious negative emotions. The emotions listed above the line are positive, ranging from mild to highly satisfying. While it is an oversimplification of our emotions, the scale is one way to think about them and understand their range. Our feelings often do not exist in a singular state. We can have simultaneous emotions—nervous but excited, frustrated and angry, happy but anxious.

On most normal days we shift periodically between mild satisfaction and mild irritation. We depend on others to pick up on our nonverbal and verbal cues, read our emotional signals along with the situational cues, and regulate or adjust their behavior to try and keep us in a calm or satisfied emotional state. It's something we all are expected to do for each other.

Use the scale to explore your own emotional responses during a short period of the day. This is a thinking exercise; you do not need to act differently based on the information. It is meant for you to reflect on your emotions, how you express them and how they may look through the eyes of others.

2. **We understand that specific situations and how people behave in those situations shape our emotions, and that we are still expected to keep the expression of our emotions under reasonable control. Figuring out how to do this is part of social problem-solving. We recognize the emotion, but that doesn't mean we emote.**
Emotions are not just irrational mood swings; usually they are produced or caused in response to situations or other people. At times we seem to wake up bending toward one type of emotion or another for no obvious reason. Most of us have had a day that started out great, only to be thrown off by some unfortunate episode—for example, our computer crashed, someone got upset with us, we never got to all the tasks we hoped to accomplish. With much of the day not fully within our control, we are at constant risk for experiencing unanticipated negative emotions.

To help manage such unplanned feelings, we learn to become emotional sailboats, adjusting our sails to keep moving in the right direction regardless of whatever storms erupt. Learning to steady our emotions is definitely an act of maturation. As teenagers we are emotional tempests (at home; not in public), but by our early twenties we are expected to be more emotionally steady—at least on the job!

A man with a lot of professional experience showed up for an appointment at our office. Previously he had been told it was canceled, but he apparently had forgotten. Upon learning he would not be seen that day, he flew into a rage that required special therapists to calm him down. The next week, when asked how he normally calmed himself down when things did not turn out as planned, he could not think of a single strategy his life had taught him to utilize in those difficult moments.

It is critically important to monitor our emotional responses and try to control them. *There is a significant difference between an emotional thought and an emotional reaction.*

Showing big emotions at work is unexpected. Those who have major mood swings, from outbursts of happiness to eruptions of outrage, appear to be emotionally unstable. These employees consistently express their strong feelings or fail to compress their emotional reactions, even around relatively small problems. This breaks one of the most important unwritten rules of the work environment: *We seek to stay calm and keep our coworkers calm, even in difficult situations.*

Our decision to express or not express our feelings, whether negative or positive, is based on how we think it will affect those around us. *Social problem-solving* doesn't always mean something is wrong; it can mean figuring out what to say or do based on what we know about the situation and the people in the situation. For example, if you and your coworkers are worried about getting laid off and you find out your job is safe, it would not be appropriate to celebrate in front of someone whose job is still at risk.

Another aspect of social problem-solving involves gauging how to process and respond to the many types of problems that can happen in a day. Assessing the size of a problem can be challenging for some. Our problems can range from something benign—a size one problem—to an almost catastrophic event—a size ten problem.

> Ben responded to a coworker's e-mail that was copied to the boss. The boss joined the communication thread, first thanking Ben for his work and then suggesting that he get more quickly to the point in his e-mails. Although most people would read the boss' suggestion as constructive criticism, Ben interpreted it to mean that his boss hated him, he was in trouble and he might lose his job after having been there just two weeks. When asked to determine the size of the problem (based on the feedback from his boss) in the range of things that can go wrong at work, Ben said, "I have no problems less than a size five!"

We are expected to react and respond to the little annoyances that come up in the day with minimal emotional arousal; these problems come in sizes one, two, three or four. They may be described more accurately as glitches and may include, to give a few examples, having to repeat what you said because someone did not hear you, getting stuck in traffic and being five minutes late to work, talking to an employee who does not seem friendly, showing up for an appointment on the wrong day or at the wrong time, or dealing with the fact that the copy machine broke yet again. We are expected to do little more than sigh over these types of inconveniences and think about how to avoid them in the future (this is part of the problem-solving process).

Problems that come in sizes five, six and seven cause us to divert significant amounts of time from the workday to resolve them. What makes for a medium-size problem is not only the energy and resources it requires, but also its potential to draw others into our negative emotional experience. Examples of these problems would be losing your passport right before an international business trip, meeting with an employee who has been acting in a way fellow team members find annoying, having to lay off an unproductive worker, or losing work you thought you'd saved on your computer but now cannot locate in any of the backup systems. As frustrating as it is to deal with these types of problems, the emotional responses they generate are still expected to be fairly benign. While our face and tone of voice will be serious to reflect how we feel, we still are not expected to react loudly when things don't go our way, showing we are really upset on our faces, in our voices or in our harsh words.

Size eight, nine and ten problems fall into the moving-toward-catastrophe category. Obvious examples are serious car accidents, natural disasters, a severe illness that hampers your ability to work or may be life-threatening or losing your job. When these problems first hit, we are allowed to express ourselves more vocally or intensely for a brief period; but even with large problems we are expected to calm our emotional response gradually and adjust to the new situation. Coworkers will understand if we have experienced something traumatic and are more reactive and less productive, but after a short period we are expected to rebound to an emotionally neutral state and return to productivity.

Regardless of the size of the problem you perceive you are experiencing, if you lash out at others you will create a new problem for yourself. If you have large emotional reactions to problems, especially when it is perceived you are taking your problem out on others in the work environment you may end up with a new problem on your hands; the fact that your supervisor or work peers are upset with you for reacting so negatively to them or others they work with.

Many adults with social learning weakness still have trouble figuring out how to judge the size of their problems in the context of a situation and how to respond so that others will continue helping them. One way to look at this is through the Problem-Solving Thermometer. Use the Problem-Solving Thermometer on the following page to help you determine an adequate gauge for life's glitches and problems.

3. **We appreciate the impact emotions play on our social memories across time.**
Emotions are memorable. What we remember mostly about people is how they made us feel. As hokey as that may seem, check out your own memories. You may have a distant recollection of someone you met at an event, but you tend to have strong memories of how you *felt*, especially if the person tipped your emotional scale positively or negatively.

Emotional memories also come in different sizes. The stronger the emotion we felt at the time, the more likely we are to remember someone associated with the memory in a positive or negative way.

While this may sound obvious, some people don't realize that emotional memories accumulate. We know that friendships are deeply tied to our emotions and related memories. The people we consider our friends are those with whom we associate a number of positive emotional memories over time. And we connect people whom we dislike with a set of negative emotional memories.

Problem-Solving Thermometer

Size of the Problem

Big Problems (8-10)

_____

_____

_____

Medium Problems (5-7)

_____

_____

_____

Small Problems (1-4)

_____

_____

_____

Not A Problem (0)

_____

_____

10
9
8
7
6
5
4
3
2
1
0

Compress to a Smaller Reaction

EMOTIONAL REACTION*

List Feelings/Reactions
(List your feelings and the ways you can react/respond in a smaller way to Medium and Small size problems.)

_____

_____

_____

Feelings and Responses for Medium Problems (compressing to a size 2-4 response/reaction):

_____

_____

Feelings and Responses for Small Problems (compressing to a size 0-1 response/reaction):

_____

_____

Not A Problem (0)

_____

_____

*Emotional Reaction
(compress emotional reaction-especially when in public)

Steve was a hard worker constantly trying to gather the latest information so he could provide additional help on projects. However, he often erred in the way he shared the information; people thought he was using it to show off. Each time his boss became perturbed with him, Steve would apologize or promise to be a better team player. But then the next week, he would do something to make a fellow employee unhappy, and his boss would have to speak to him again. Steve felt satisfied each week that he had appeared to resolve the issue, but he didn't realize that the boss was accumulating a set of social-emotional memories that reflected poorly on Steve, and that ultimately he did not consider Steve a good employee, regardless of how diligently he worked.

4. **We all are born egocentric, focused on our own needs. Our egos are the lens through which we view the world, helping us to make sense of things as we interpret other people's actions and discern their meaning.** Because our egos also represent our self-interest, we may become easily offended by others or wary of their actions. But as we mature socially, we are expected to refrain from expressing all of our thoughts and feelings about the people around us. These remain mostly private, and only we know how we truly think and feel. This keeps others feeling OK in our presence.

Even if we are being polite, we still consider our own needs. But at the same time, we modify our behavior to show we are also considering what other people need and expect from us.

For example, women often have to wait in line to use a public bathroom. They stand in line because they recognize that other people have needs as well.

If someone pushed ahead, she would be perceived as rude, disrespectful or insensitive. So even though their own needs are what propel them to the bathroom in the first place, the women defer to others' needs once they are waiting in line. The social mind is a complicated place.

In novels, authors often explain a character's thoughts and emotions. In *The Historian* by Elizabeth Kostova (2005), a teenager narrates her own thoughts and what she perceives to be her father's thoughts.

"He said he just didn't know if it was a good idea for me to go [on the trip], since these talks promised to be rather—tense. It might not be quite—but he couldn't go on and I knew why. Just as I could not use my real argument for going to Oxford [to visit], he could not use his for wanting to prevent me from going. I could not tell him aloud that I couldn't bear to let him, with his dark-circled eyes and the fatigued stoop of shoulder and head, out of my sight now. And he could not counter aloud that he might not be safe in Oxford and that, therefore, I might not be safe with him. He was silent for a minute or two, and then he asked me very gently what we were having for dessert…"

All communication is motive-based, and people around us interpret every single one of our actions and words and try to figure out our intentions, even if we aren't communicating directly with them. When we communicate with language, we don't always say exactly what we mean. We choose our words carefully to help craft our message in a way we want it to be understood or implied. Still, people will read between the lines and gather their own conclusions.

You can see how a divide between intention and interpretation might lead to misunderstandings.

Allen, a 30-year-old computer professional in New York, did not have a good track record keeping jobs, even though he was competent in his work. He expressed with great frustration that he had very good intentions but that people "did not get" him. He believed he was helping customers by teaching them to find the answers themselves, directing them to relevant Web sites or materials they could read on their own. Allen's boss told him customers had complained and he needed to provide them with actual service. But Allen insisted his way was better in the long run. He summarized his experiences trying to understand people and their social demands by exclaiming, "People are idiots!"

Each of us wants to be respected for what we are trying to accomplish during the workday. We attempt to "mind-read" and interpret the meaning of people's actions. We then have an associated emotional response. If we feel someone's actions are meant to be helpful, we feel reasonably good about that person. When we feel someone might be acting with ill intent or suspicious motives, we start to put on our emotional armor and feel defensive.

Curt decided unilaterally to change a five-point plan his boss had established for an overseas business trip, but Curt did not inform his boss about the change during their daily phone calls. Later, Curt recognized his boss was upset by his actions (which he continued to try and justify), but he failed to notice a deeper level of distrust brewing. The boss agreed to meet with Curt the day after he returned home, but then canceled the appointment at the last minute. Curt arranged a meeting for the following day and the boss again canceled. This pattern of arranged meetings and cancellations continued for the entire workweek. Curt was upset and felt disrespected by his boss. What Curt did not understand, until it was explained to him, was that the boss in fact felt disrespected by Curt. From the boss's point of view, Curt had acted as if he knew better and could "one-up" the boss when he was in a foreign country. Although the reality was that Curt meant no disrespect, the boss's perception of Curt's actions made him angry.

Because people often mask their intentions and emotions, our minds attempt to seek meaning for just about every action—and lack of action.

As mentioned at the start of this book, our social radar system seeks to find hidden meaning in what is *not* said or not done, just as much as we search for meaning in what *is* said and done!

5. **We understand that humans share common emotional responses, allowing us with some accuracy to imagine or empathize with how people feel and what they expect.**
In our attempts to conceal our thoughts and desires, we may not state what we would like to happen or how we feel. In fact, at times we go to the opposite extreme, saying we don't want something that we really do want, to encourage people not to make a big deal about us. This is common when it comes to discussing birthday celebrations. When a friend asks what you want for your birthday, it is usually expected that you say, "Thanks, but I don't want for anything."

> Recently, an aquantance of ours had a baby about a month before her own birthday. When the time came, and her husband asked what she wanted for her birthday, she said the baby was gift enough, providing everything she could ever want. When her husband didn't give her a gift on her

birthday, she called her mother in tears; she did not really mean she didn't want anything at all!

* * *

When a young adult in our clinic was encouraged to listen to what people were saying and to acknowledge their feelings, he said, "But I can't know how they feel, because I am not them!" When we shared with him that most people have similar emotional reactions to similar events, and that allows us to predict and respond to how other people are feeling, he asked, "How come no one ever told me that before?"

A point reiterated throughout this book is that work relationships — all our relationships — *are* emotional relationships. Our coworkers not only expect us to have job-related knowledge and competency, but they also expect us to relate to and get along with them. It is expected that we actually *work* to figure people out and understand—their thoughts and feelings.

To relate to people means we detect and respond to emotional situations or to the emotions themselves, ones we imagine our colleagues are experiencing. This task is made all the harder by the fact that people generally conceal their emotions in the workplace. They may even lie to try and persuade us they are fine when they are not. Nonetheless, it is expected that we understand enough about the social world to predict people's emotional responses in a given situation.

Empathy involves relating to what we perceive others are feeling, based on our own emotional experiences or knowledge of the world.

Understanding that we share similar emotional reactions to similar problems helps us to empathize. If someone gets in a fender bender on the way to work, we imagine it is frustrating but not devastating, and we might offer supportive words. If we find out someone's daughter has been accepted into her college of choice, we would guess that the parent is happy and excited for his daughter because of our own memories of what it felt like to be accepted to college, and we'd offer our congratulations. Other events, such as a terrorist attack or a major earthquake, are extremely upsetting to most people, so we could understand how others might be feeling and share our own feelings accordingly.

6. **We learn to recognize nonverbal and verbal cues to intuit other people's emotions and better appreciate their perspective. People usually do not explicitly tell us how they feel; instead they expect us to try and interpret their emotions using the very subtle cues they provide, based on our understanding of emotional compression.**

> Larry, a talented marketing specialist in his late thirties with an Ivy League education, struggled to recognize people's feelings. Often he was upset by how his peers treated him, but he failed to read their verbal and nonverbal cues. When he was explaining a project, his exceptional attention to detail actually was tedious and quite annoying to his colleagues, but Larry didn't see this because he wasn't able to read their reactions or emotions accurately.

While we are often quick to tell people what we did during a day, we are not quick to share our feelings. And as pointed out previously, we are less likely to show our true emotions in the workplace. Our emotions are something that we privately own; they allow us to be privately ourselves, even when surrounded by people.

On the other hand, most of us are born with a unique curiosity and social radar system we use to figure out other people's emotions. Even if they aren't talking about their feelings directly, we take our cues from what they say, what they fail to say, their tone of voice, eye contact, rate of speech, breathing patterns, gestures, facial expressions, general physical appearance and signs of physical stress or calm as we simultaneously and rapidly interpret and infer what people really mean or feel.

Carrie spoke to her boss using straightforward, informational language, but her tone of voice implied that she was angry. The other employees stopped what they were doing upon hearing Carrie's harsh tone and asked each other why she was so mad.

Attempting to interpret each other's emotions is as much a part of the workday as doing our actual jobs. However, some people are not able to extract this information intuitively. For them, the multitasking required to intuit another person's social-emotional mind is overwhelming; therefore, they tend to dismiss its importance. Or (as explained earlier in the discussion on emotional compression) they did not intuitively learn that emotional expression becomes compressed in our teenage and adult years, and that we have to look for far more nuanced, subtle facial expressions, gestures and tone of voice to interpret more precisely how people think and feel. If people who do not perceive these nuances are perceived as indifferent to others' emotions, they may brush off any negative reaction, saying, "I did what I was asked to do, so I don't know why that person is mad. I guess he's just having a bad day."

A number of people had gone to Mark's boss to complain about Mark not being a team player.

He seemed self-absorbed in his work and took other people's time without showing appreciation. Meanwhile, Mark voiced his own complaints about a colleague who was not helping with a work project. When Mark came into our clinic, we asked him what he thought the boss was feeling while listening to Mark's complaint. He said the boss was concurring that the colleague was difficult to work with. When we then asked Mark to consider how the boss was acting at the time (not using eye contact, packing up his work bag and walking to his car while Mark continued to talk), it became clear that Mark was not reading the nonverbal cues and that the boss was expressing frustration with Mark's inability to relate socially to his coworkers.

Reading other people's emotions may be like trying to zero in on a moving target, but no matter how complicated, it cannot be dismissed or trivialized. Instead, everyone needs "emotional target practice" to figure out people's feelings. Children begin this practice through daily play. Research demonstrates that preschool students who are emotionally well regulated and sensitive to understanding and reacting to others' emotions are the most likely to do well in school. Adults with social learning weaknesses may not have a history of practicing social interactions through spontaneous play. As children, they may have been absorbed in a book or building remarkable block towers instead of playing with other children. Their limited early social interactions provided little practice and therefore less experience exploring how to read and react to others' social minds.

Ryan had a successful career as a computer specialist. The fifty-year-old worked well with his peers and had never had a negative job review. But his work required him to problem-solve computer programming issues, with little time left to interact with coworkers other than in meetings. When he was forty, he met the woman he eventually married—and discovered his lack of practice in social interaction. Discussions at work were nearly always topic-based, but with his wife, conversations were supposed to show that he cared about her. Ryan was stumped. He had years of practice talking about computers, but little experience using language to show he was thinking about someone's emotional well-being. His wife expected him to ask about her day to show he was interested in her life; otherwise, she felt he didn't care about her. But Ryan explained to me that he had demonstrated his commitment to his wife by marrying her, and that was all he felt was needed to show he cared. He did not understand how asking her about her day mattered. As we began to work on language-based strategies to show his wife he was interested in her emotionally, he said he literally had almost no practice in talking to people, even as a child. Instead of hanging out with his peers, he found his peace by going to the library every day and reading during lunch and other breaks in the school day.

7. **We adapt our verbal and nonverbal behavior according to how we imagine those around us are feeling.**
   As we interpret people's emotions, we also need to adjust our behavior accordingly. Those who are seen as sensitive, empathetic or friendly are not only able to recognize someone's feeling state but can adapt to it as well.

   A coworker who lets you know, directly or indirectly, that he is sad or overwhelmed due to an impending divorce, financial issues or work problems expects you to relate to his feelings, either with a respectful nonverbal response (looking sad) or a related verbal response such as, "Been there, and that sucks."

On the flip side, if he expresses that he's feeling good and *you* are the one in a funk, you still are expected to produce a positive or enthusiastic response to show that you connect with his feelings, even if you don't feel positive yourself.

> A group of young adults worked together in a social thinking group to explore others' social thinking and related social skills. Nick coordinated a get-together after one of the weekly groups, in large part to celebrate his birthday. Although everyone agreed to send confirmation e-mails the week before the event, none did. Furthermore, all were late to the group the day of the get-together, leading Nick to believe that they didn't like him and didn't want to come to the celebration. When they arrived at the group session, none acknowledged Nick's plans or his birthday. Nick was clearly upset. Once we pointed out how Nick had interpreted their lack of action, Sarah groaned and apologized, saying she "felt terrible" and was "embarrassed." Joe did not speak up, and when asked how he felt about making Nick feel bad, he replied, "Indifferent." Nick tried to cover his increasing anger through humor, pretending he was going to punch Joe. When Joe was told that saying he was indifferent indicated he didn't care about Nick and would be seen as a freeloader at the party, Joe responded, "Why would I want to be like Sarah and feel miserable just to match what Nick is feeling?"

Although it may seem odd, relating to someone else's sadness is usually an initial step in making that person feel better. If people feel they are understood, then they are better prepared to move on emotionally. If people feel they are not heard, their emotions can get stuck or spiral into further darkness.

In fact, one "good social skill" is simply showing you are listening to someone talk by nodding your head and occasionally saying "Wow," "Uh-huh" or "That's a bummer," depending on the nature of the message being relayed. If you fail to give this type of social-emotional feedback in the form of small comments or nonverbal responses, the person might feel you are not really listening. Even a response as simple as a furrowed eyebrow can demonstrate how you are empathizing with the person's story. It can go a long way toward conveying that you are relating to someone emotionally!

8. **We recognize that how other people feel and express their feelings can influence how we ourselves feel and react.**
As mentioned earlier in this chapter, emotional contagion is an active part of our emotional processing system. We can easily bring each other down or lift each others' spirits, just by expressing our emotions in a negative or positive way.

Most people try to keep an upper hand on their emotional responses because they understand intuitively that their behavior affects how others respond to them.

"Misery loves company," the saying goes, but realistically there are limits to how much people want to share in the misery of others. We seek out those who leave us feeling pretty good, or at least not bad. People who are known to wallow in their own misery and sorrows have difficulty attracting company. And revealing sad or negative feelings too often can lead to social rejection.

Shari was forty-five when I began to work with her at my clinic. One of the first things she said about herself was that there was "an invisible sign posted on my back that says, 'My name is Shari and your job is to not talk to me.'" Shari knew she had difficulty with appropriate social skills but had no idea what that meant. As we began to work with Shari, she expressed enthusiasm that someone was finally going to "teach her social skills," and she agreed to do weekly social thinking homework. However, each time we tried to introduce a new concept, she would say, "You have to understand how bad my life is." When we encouraged her to explore the concepts, she escalated her emotional response by yelling, "You're just like everyone else; you don't care about me either!" Regardless of how much we tried to explain how thinking about others' perspectives and emotions could help her better relate to people, she insisted on expressing her frustrations, even if it meant she had to yell to get people to listen.

Clearly, Shari's insistence on sharing her misery caused people to avoid her. While some might stay and listen to her tales of woe, few if any would return to talk to her again (the impact of social-emotional memory). Even her devoted parents asked that she not come to the family's Easter celebration that year. The blatant rejections fueled Shari's unhappiness, making her lash out more. She lost her job due to poor customer relations.

Frustrated with Shari's personal tirades each time we worked with her, we informed her about a rule in communication: You don't tell people what they already know about you. Her homework assignment was to write down everything she thought we already knew about her life. Dutifully, she returned the next week with a list of all the frustrations she had previously shared. She then said, "I figured out that you already know about my hard life, and if I want you to help me get better I have to focus on what you have to teach me and not tell you what you already know about me." Remarkably, Shari kept her word and never screamed at us again about not understanding her life. She also slowly made inroads with her parents, spending time relating to their feelings rather than obsessing on her own negative cycle. Eventually she was able to get a new job, which she's kept for a number of years, having learned that just because she gets upset, she should not always share her frustrations with others.

9. **We know that friends are people who make us feel good about ourselves over time. Those who make us feel good in the moment are friendly acquaintances but not necessarily friends. Those about whom we have negative emotional memories are not our friends—and some of them may even be our adversaries.**

Forming friendships at work is expected. Establishing positive acquaintances is the norm. Avoiding adversarial relationships is important to job satisfaction as well as potential growth within the company.

Maintaining friendships at work and spending time with colleagues after work (golfing, drinking, going to movies) are two types of networking. Social networks—the old-fashioned kind—introduce you to a broader social world. One person tells someone else something positive about you, and that person tells another, and so on. Paying attention to different aspects of your emotions can help you form these important social networks and be more emotionally satisfied with your job.

However, even if you do not develop social networks or friendships, that does not mean your colleagues have no social-emotional thoughts about you. In fact, if you are consistently the source of negative social memories, you can get a negative reputation. We humans have a nasty habit of sharing our feelings when we feel someone has acted wrongly. Most of us don't blab about how good someone made us feel, but it is very common to go and tell a few close coworkers when we feel someone at work has mistreated us. Gossiping about people's social-emotional missteps is an unfortunate aspect of our humanity and makes it more difficult for people to redeem themselves after they've been branded as difficult, unfriendly or self-important.

Deborah was a motivated teacher dedicated to helping students with learning differences. She went out of her way to do the best job possible, but she consistently struggled to maintain harmonious relations with her colleagues. She worked diligently with her students and advocated for their needs with fellow teachers and principals. The only thing missing was an ability to relate to her coworkers. Deborah's first misstep was in the way she presented her report and recommendations for specific students, without acknowledging or showing appreciation for the efforts of fellow teachers who had worked with the students. It got so bad that they filed complaints, saying they felt Deborah did not listen to them and did not respect their points of view. Deborah's second misstep came when she met with the principal; instead of relating emotionally (showing remorse and discussing ways in which she could let the teachers know she appreciated their efforts), she began to cry and defend her position logically. The principal interpreted her behavior as defensive because her argument did not acknowledge being wrong, nor did she give any credit to her colleagues. Deborah's tears and attempts to get the principal to agree with her point of view resulted in further misunderstandings. The principal filed her own complaint, calling Deborah rude and insubordinate. Deborah was put on probation for one year with the stipulation that if her social skills don't improve, she will lose her job. Keep in mind, no one ever complained about the actual work she was doing with the students.

The work environment can be highly emotional, each day requiring us to tiptoe through an emotional minefield. The field is more perilous if you were not born with a strong emotional intelligence and cannot depend on your intuition to guide you. However, it is possible to improve your social-emotional mind or social radar system and adapt your behavior by relying on your other intelligences to feed you information and then practicing what you learn.

In the coming chapters, we will continue to explore emotions and how they are woven through all of our communication—whether it's figuring out what other people are thinking, knowing what behavior is expected from one situation to the next, or recognizing your emotional responses. Next we'll look at perspective taking, one of the foundations of social thinking and an integral piece of the social puzzle.

Good Intentions Are Not Good Enough

POINTS TO CONSIDER

- ❖ Emotions are not just irrational mood swings; usually they are produced or caused by situations or other people

- ❖ With much of the day not fully within our control, we are at constant risk for experiencing unanticipated negative emotions.

- ❖ Attempting to interpret each other's emotions is as much a part of the workday as doing our actual jobs.

- ❖ To manage unplanned feelings, we learn to become emotional sailboats, adjusting our sails to keep moving in the right direction regardless of whatever storms erupt.

> "An intelligent person is never afraid or ashamed
> to find errors in his understanding of things."
> ~ Bryant H. McGill

Chapter 4

Perspective Taking
Are You Thinking What I'm Thinking?

Social thinking recognizes that we negotiate virtually everything we do through an almost imperceptible thought process that considers other points of view, or perspectives, in addition to our own. This practice is at the heart of social thinking, and it is one of the finest balancing acts we perform on a daily basis.

Perspective taking is like many social concepts—it's easy to get a sense of its general meaning but hard to define precisely. Simply put, it is the ability to look at things from a perspective other than our own. But of course a concept in theory is not the same as a concept in practice. The reality is that in communication we have to deal with many things happening at once. We must think about and respond to an amazing amount of information, all in a very short period of time.

We process and respond not only to our own thoughts and feelings, but also to what we believe other people are thinking and feeling. When we express our opinions or point of view, we gauge our responses to minimize social conflict and maximize social harmony, so that others do not feel threatened or disrespected.

Our ability to handle this kind of social complexity is even more incredible in light of the fact that a neurotypical brain can process and respond to an array of social information in a tiny amount of time—from milliseconds to two seconds. In other words, it is not enough to just figure out someone else's perspective;

you also have to do it very quickly. Watch people interact, and you will observe rapid-fire responses that are coded both verbally and nonverbally.

One important area of research related to perspective-taking is theory of mind, defined as the ability to attribute mental states to other humans—to understand that they have thoughts, beliefs, desires and intentions that may be different from ours (Baron-Cohen, 2000). The neurotypical mind develops this aptitude by ages four to six learning intuitively that *your thoughts are different from my thoughts.*

Theory of mind developed after psychologists studied how chimpanzees lived together in a community and observed them using a social-emotional thought process to help dictate their actions with others. This observation took on a new life of study for researchers, who sought to learn more about humans born to weak social understanding, such as those with autism spectrum disorder (ASD). As a result of this area of study, scientists and academics have been better able to compare the thinking of people with social learning challenges and those perceived as having good social skills.

Like most any process related to social thinking, perspective-taking is multidimensional, synergistic and dynamic. It happens not only during intentional or planned interactions, but also spontaneously in the spaces people share. An overview of what we are expected to do when taking perspective follows.

THE SEVEN CORE TENETS OF PERSPECTIVE TAKING

1. **THOUGHTS** We think about people whether or not we plan to interact with them. When we are in the presence of others, we cannot help but think about what they might be thinking. We notice what they're looking at, what they're doing, where they're going. This begins the process of deciding whether we want to interact or, on a more basic level, whether we feel safe or comfortable in their presence.

   The process begins by looking at the other person's eyes to figure out what he might be looking at and therefore thinking about. This skill develops intuitively in most children right around the time they reach their first birthday and is known as *joint attention*.

If we do plan to talk to someone, then we think more concretely about whether this is a good time, whether the person is distracted or perhaps already talking to someone else and similar concerns. This awareness can help us to figure out if it's okay to speak and add our own thoughts.

2. EMOTIONS Although our emotions are philosophically different from our thoughts, the two are deeply entwined. We can talk about them differently, but they generally operate best together, much like an iPod is most useful with ear buds.

   Some of us may like to believe that our emotional selves are present only in personal relationships and that our intellectual selves take over during the workday, but that is not the case. Emotions, as we learned in Chapter 3, are as much a part of the workday as the concrete or practical aspects of our jobs. In fact, the idea of a *team player* is more about how people relate to each other than about the knowledge they bring to the job.

3. PHYSICAL MOTIVES AND INTENTIONS Most of us are pretty good at reading physical intentions, meaning we can determine what people are planning to do next based on how we perceive their movements and the direction of their gaze. We think we know why someone is heading into the bathroom or going into the office kitchen, without specifically being told his needs or desires. Reading people's physical intentions helps us to determine their motives. Unconsciously and consciously, we track the behavior of those around us to try and figure out what they are doing. Reading their movements helps us to determine what they are thinking and planning.

   This skill is used not only to figure out the plans and actions of people we know; it is also critical for handling many daily life skills, such as driving a car or crossing a street.

These complex tasks would be impossible if we weren't able to anticipate the actions or intentions of drivers or know whether they were thinking about us as we prepared to cross a street.

Our brains assist us in these endeavors by providing a social radar system that helps determine people's motives and intentions, even when we are not taking specific or direct notice of those around us. This is especially true in the relatively small physical spaces many of us share at work. You do notice your coworkers' comings and goings, but their movements may not attract your attention until they walk right up to you.

4. **LANGUAGE-BASED MEANING AND INTENTIONS** The way people speak is often indirect, requiring us to intuit the actual meaning of their words. What a person says is not necessarily what he means. We try to figure it out, in the same way we try to determine someone's thoughts and plans by observing the direction of their gaze and their physical movements.

A client asked me to explain why old friends or acquaintances who run into each other often end their conversation by saying, "Let's get together soon," but they rarely follow through. I offered two ways to interpret this. One is that the people are being polite but really don't want to spend extra time with each other. The other meaning could be that they wish they had time to spend together, but their schedules are too full. Either way it can be taken as a compliment, because they are saying they would like to see each other again—even if they don't make the time for it!

Relating to people can be like a social-emotional chess game, with each of us trying to predict someone else's strategy and deciding our next move, based on our perception of what we think that person is thinking.

In the workplace, when groups work cooperatively, each team member has to take into account every other person's needs to figure out how to complement or add to each other's efforts, rather than detract from them.

> Evan felt the team was not supporting an important point he had made. He confided this to a colleague, who assured Evan he would support him at the next team meeting. However, Evan later reported in great frustration that the colleague did not make his support evident, and instead indicated that he thought other people had good ideas as well. Evan did not realize that to share ideas on teams, there is a fair amount of "social-emotional jockeying." You need to make other team members feel as if you value their opinions before you're in a position to get them to fully consider your point of view.

What we decide to say or not say requires us to interpret what the other person is saying and doing.

Sometimes what is *not* said can be more powerful than what *is* said, and this comes into play when interpreting meaning and intentions through language. Ever notice what happens when a journalist interviews a politician and tries to ask a difficult question to get the person to reveal something the public has not heard? Listen carefully to the response of the politician; he begins by acting as if he is answering the question, but then he transitions to a different topic to circumvent the suggested one. It is done with such art that many times listeners don't realize the politician just sidestepped giving an answer altogether.

5. **BELIEF SYSTEMS** Stomping on or disregarding a belief system is one of the quickest ways to irritate or upset someone you work with. There are many kinds of belief systems—cultural, gender-based, work-related, religious, financial, educational and political, to name several.

As adults we respect that people have different belief systems and we avoid treading in those areas when relating to each other. Again, this means knowing what *not* to say just as much as knowing *what* to say.

When it comes to jokes, be aware that just because you think a joke is hilarious, you can't tell it without considering whether it would offend other people and their belief systems, even if they are only overhearing it. We are expected to remain highly attuned to the fact that our coworkers may not share our personal philosophies or views of the world.

If people tell jokes that make fun of their *own* belief system, it doesn't mean you can then tell those jokes to someone else. In other words, you can make jokes about your belief system but not other people's. If I am Jewish and you are not, you shouldn't tell me a Jewish joke. However, if both of us are Jewish and we are friends, then it's probably OK to tell the joke. Clearly these are hidden rules and have to be well understood before attempting to discuss or share your beliefs or humor in the work environment.

At times communication really is that complicated. There are few hard-and-fast rules about what you can or can't say. Instead, you must interpret the information you gather from all these different angles of perspective taking. If you aren't sure whether you can get away with a comment or joke, don't even try. And don't think you can tell a joke or behave a certain way just because you saw a colleague at work saying or doing the same. There are jokes that another person in the office can get away with telling; you may not be so lucky.

6. **PRIOR KNOWLEDGE AND EXPERIENCES** What you know about a person or situation is critical for determining what to do or say.

Consider the different approaches to giving instructions to a colleague who has shared many of the same work experiences that you have, versus a new hire who doesn't know much about your work environment. In the first case, you would give minimal information, figuring the other person already has the same basic knowledge as you do; in the second case you would give detailed instructions because you know the new hire has limited experience working at the company.

Our minds are like human global positioning systems, trying to find their way around information to keep communications moving forward efficiently.

In fact, our brains are set up to be highly efficient in relating to each other. That's why when we fail to give enough information, or we provide too much, people can quickly become irritated with the way we are communicating. They expect us to know enough about them, or at least about the specific situation, to avoid such mistakes most of the time. If you are standing in line with a coworker at the bank, you assume she is there to deal with her money. In this situation you would not ask, even to be friendly, "So what are you doing here—your banking?" Instead you can make a comment about something less obvious, such as—"This line is moving slowly, I hope we're not late getting back to work."

Keep in mind that we all make mistakes at times, sharing too much or too little information. If you think you might be sharing too much information, you can always preface your comments with, "Stop me if you already know this." Listeners also have ways of alerting you if they are familiar with what you're saying, slipping in a comment such as, "Oh, yeah, I've already heard that," which sends a cue that you should skip to another, less familiar part of the story.

7. **PERSONALITY** We can enjoy relating to all kinds of people. However, the particular way in which we relate to someone has to do in part with how we perceive that individual's personality. A coworker who is more cerebral might bring out the intellectual side of our personality, while we may share our funny side with someone who we know is more playful, especially during a more relaxed time.

The bottom line is that, to some extent, we are expected

to be social chameleons, modifying our behavior according to the people, the situation and how we would best relate. If we do not adapt in this fashion, our behavior could be thought of as odd or it could make people feel uncomfortable—for instance, if we act overly polite or too informal in situations that do not call for such behaviors.

Andy, who was in his early twenties, was recently employed in an entry level job, working for a small company in the shipping and receiving office. While many of Andy's coworkers were also young men who acted "cool" when they spoke to each other, they adapted their behavior to be more formal in the presence of managers. While Andy was working at his desk one day, the CEO walked in. Andy looked up, tossed his chin in the air to greet the CEO with a head nod, and said, "Yo, what's up, dude?" Andy's coworkers laughed at him, knowing it was not the appropriate way to greet the head of the company, even though the work culture was very casual.

PUTTING IT ALL TOGETHER
IS WHAT'S EXPECTED WHEN TAKING PERSPECTIVE

Perspective-taking is never linear, orderly or sequenced. Figuring out someone's mind can be quite a dance. We sidestep what we perceive as potential emotional hotspots and try to maneuver toward areas where we can agree and be comfortable together.

However, because we do not always say exactly what we are thinking, often the path of communication can be circuitous.

Perspective-taking is something like the circus act where the performer sets a bunch of plates spinning one by one on separate poles and then has to keep them going, watching and running from pole to pole to prevent a crash.

The practice of perspective-taking has the greatest potential impact on our ability to relate well to others. It can help us figure out how to modify our response according to how others think, and ensure a predictable emotional response from them. This does not mean we must constantly seek to please; on the contrary, our responses at times can cause disappointment or frustration—for instance, if we make a decision at work and someone else disagrees with it.

Many adults with social learning weaknesses can fully understand each of the perspective-taking tenets, but may find their brains are inefficient in processing all this information simultaneously. It can also be challenging to determine the most important thing to focus on in a particular interaction.

> Todd developed a friendship with a coworker based on their common interests. Shortly afterward, the coworker fell out of favor with her superiors. Todd was worried about losing his job due to upcoming budget cuts. We advised him not to engage in banter with the coworker in the presence of their superiors, because it was possible they would associate Todd too closely with the co-worker and perceive Todd in a similarly negative way.

In this example, there were hidden rules specific to this situation that did not apply to situations outside of the work environment (for example, if the coworker and Todd ran into each other outside of work). Every situation has its own implied set of social behaviors and expectations, and they are rarely discussed or explained. Employees can receive negative reviews for not recognizing and following the hidden rules, without ever getting a proper explanation as to what they did wrong; they are just expected not to do it again!

> Jacob wanted a letter of recommendation from a professor at his university. Jacob had worked closely with the professor and felt he was a friend. Jacob also believed that one of his many strengths was his persistence; therefore, when he didn't hear back from the professor, Jacob repeatedly contacted

him to ask if he had written the letter yet. Apparently the professor had not; Jacob persisted with requests. When the professor finally sent the letter, it was very negative. Jacob felt hurt and upset. Only later did he understand that bugging his professor about the letter had created a negative social memory. The professor was unable to focus on Jacob's positive qualities and strengths and was only able to see his weaknesses.

Although relating to our coworkers is of prime importance for effective teamwork, how to do so is not made explicit. We are just supposed to *know* how to behave when the CEO is present at an important meeting versus at a company barbecue. The behavioral expectations are established largely by the situation and what is known about the people within it.

The complexity of the perspective-taking process is difficult for all, but with practice we grow in competency. This constant but subtle mind-reading—assessing every situation and taking perspective of people whose paths we cross—can be at times highly accurate and at other times fraught with error. Interpreting and responding to others does not involve black-and-white decision-making, but instead operates in a gray area in which we must constantly handle multiple variables. Our social judgments are based not on the firm foundation of science, but instead on the shaky ground of social interpretation. That's why we refer to many of our mistakes as human error or "just being human."

Because we all make mistakes, people can be somewhat forgiving—to a point. As detailed in the previous chapter, we have very active social-emotional memories that store information about people we encounter repeatedly; more important, we remember how these people make us feel overall. If they make us feel good across time, then the relationship is likely to develop. But if our social memories bring up negative or neutral emotions, then we will probably avoid relating to them (and we won't always remember exactly why).

Persons who are more comfortable with hard data and

empirical evidence may have difficulty accepting the concept of social thinking as a formula used to produce better social skills. Scientists or those in fields such as math or engineering may find the ideas of social interpretation, perspective-taking and emotional responses flaky and too difficult to quantify to take seriously. Ironically, this book is written for many of these people.

People in the hard sciences are not the first to discount the importance of social thinking. In fact, in the late 1950's, David Weschler, the influential psychologist who created what still remains one of the most widely used measures of IQ, decided to exclude the measurement of "social intelligence" seeing it merely as "general intelligence applied to social situations." While Social intelligence shows itself abundantly in the nursery, on the playground, in barracks and factories and salesrooms, it eludes the formal standardized conditions of the testing laboratory.[1]

Thinking consciously about our social behavior—especially when for most people it is signed, sealed and delivered with little conscious thought—is a confusing and often frustrating experience for those not born with a strong intuitive social navigator. Nevertheless, it appears that the ability to relate to peers and coworkers is a key indicator of vocational success (Bronson, 2000). So as fluffy as all these social thinking concepts may appear to some, few would question the importance of social behavior in relating well to others.

Working to define these elusive concepts can help us learn about our social operating systems, which can move us in a more positive direction—not only with our coworkers but our family and friends as well. Many people can report successes in their chosen professions, but few proclaim the same confidence about their social skills. Social relationships always have significant room for improvement. And so we will keep breaking down these social thinking concepts to bring what's "hidden" out into the open.

---

1 Goleman, Daniel. 2006. *Social Intelligence: The New Science of Human Relationships*. Bantam.

POINTS TO CONSIDER

❖ Our social judgments are based not on the firm foundation of science, but instead on the shaky ground of social interpretation. That's why we refer to many of our mistakes as human error or "just being human."

> "Don't knock the weather; nine-tenths of the people couldn't start a conversation if it didn't change once in a while."
>
> ~ Kin Hubbard

Chapter 5

The Four Steps of Communication
Talking Isn't the Only Way to Connect

Communication doesn't start with words. Most of the time it doesn't even end with words. We look, we move, we talk, we listen. When dealing with people face-to-face, communication is a multisystem function.

Have you ever met someone who appears just to be *downloading* information to you, not really paying attention to who you are or showing interest in what you've got to say? That person may feel like he's communicating, but in reality he's having a communication systems failure. He's not making an emotional connection or noticing the different social cues and hidden rules, that are necessary ingredients for successful interactions.

The process of interpersonal communication has at least four basic steps. They work together and play off each other. We call these the four steps of communication.

THE FOUR STEPS OF COMMUNICATION

1. **Think about the people with whom you want to communicate.**

2. **Use your body to establish a physical presence.**

3. **Use your eyes to think about people as you relate to them.**

4. **Use your words to relate to people when you talk to them.**

When first approaching a person to communicate, these four steps generally happen in order. However, we process and respond to all of the information during the entire time we are engaging with another person. We are required to be social multitaskers, and to do this we continuously process, interpret and respond to every cue almost instantaneously. If we don't react quickly—usually within about a second—people may become impatient because our communication feels too slow or laborious.

Most human brains are well-equipped for this fast-paced social interpretation and response system, but some of us lack the necessary neurological connections for the task, even if we are brilliant in other aspects of our lives.

Many of our clients have problems entering a group or figuring out what to do when they're not talking. Winner developed this four-step model to show how communication involves the whole body and is not simply focused on language. The four steps are the same no matter what the situation or interaction. We may make subtle but significant changes in the way we use our bodies, our eyes or our language to communicate, depending on the reasons for the interaction, but we still engage in these four steps simultaneously for effective communication.

THE FIRST STEP:
Think About the People With Whom You Want to Communicate

Before you begin talking to someone, many things have to happen to make the communication successful. The first step is figuring out who you're talking to and why or—if you don't know the person—establishing what you may know about him based on the situation and how you think he is feeling about the interaction. Much has already been explained in the previous chapter about perspective-taking—processing and responding to your own thoughts and feelings and the thoughts and feelings of others—that relates to this first step of communication.

Although speed is essential in the moment, before you get into a conversation it can be helpful to think briefly about what you want to say and how you want to say it. This is especially true for any anticipated interaction that you feel concerned or stressed about; the better you plan out how to deliver your message the smoother the communication is likely to be. You also spend time (if only a few seconds) thinking about what you know or don't know about the person.

Remarkably, the social brain is a pretty organized place. We have systems for keeping track of people we've met, and we store information about them similarly to the way we organize files on our computer. When we know people, our brain opens a *file* about them, providing information about who they are, their abilities, preferences, likes and dislikes, and so on. This feeds us some of the data we need for a conversation.

However, our systems can get overloaded with all of this information. Almost immediately, the files of information about others begin to fade, and we aren't able to track and access everything we've ever known about everyone we've ever encountered. We've all forgotten the name of someone we met before. The social information we acquire over our lives is just too cumbersome to keep in order. That's why we make allowances for each other's memory lapses by asking for little reminders. "I'm sorry, your name's on the tip of my tongue, but I can't remember it. I know you work in sales." (Hint: It's always good to show people that you remember *something* about them).

Even if it's the first time you're having a conversation with someone at the office, you still can think about what you might know about the person or have in common—you may work for the same company, you could both live in the same community, and you may share interests about the local scene (sports, arts, nature). That gives you some starting material for the conversation.

What you are never expected to do is go up and just begin talking to someone without any thought about what might bring you together. While you may think you're just being friendly, people will have uncomfortable thoughts if they can't figure out why you are trying to connect with them, or if they feel you aren't personally interested in them and just want to use them for their information. That's why everyone should be taking perspective and trying to figure out each other's motives, as well as how our interactions make others feel.

> Dennis came to his new job with ambitious goals, determined to exceed expectations. To learn the culture of his work environment, he met with several of the managers, explained his goals, asked detailed questions and absorbed information about how to be an effective employee. At least, that's what he thought he was doing. In reality, he was taking too much time from the managers without showing any interest in connecting to them personally. He was so focused on his own agenda, he never considered that he needed to get to know the people a bit more on a personal level if he was going to be working long term with them. Over time, fewer and fewer people were willing to give him their time. He got a bad reputation among some of the higher-ups and had to explore what he was doing that was ticking them off. His immediate supervisor said he came across as not very friendly and recommended he spend more time trying to relate to his coworkers personally and not make all of his conversations be about his job or his work goals.

Thinking about people, both before and while we're with them, is very important. But that alone does not make for successful communication. To put our thoughts into action effectively, we require assistance from our body, our eyes and our words—the three steps of communication that follow.

THE SECOND STEP:
Use Your Body to Establish a Physical Presence

While our social minds should be actively seeking information about the people we're talking to, our bodies have as much to do with communication as our thoughts and language. How we physically enter and sustain ourselves in a group is critical to how others perceive and react to us.

> Jack was a polite forty-year-old who held an important technical job. He met with us at our clinic and asked us to explain why no one would let him talk during team meetings. He was handed a set of building blocks he was told to show us how people were seated at the meeting. He put out a long block to represent the table, and three smaller blocks to represent people sitting at the ends of the table and across from him.
>
> He then put out a block to represent himself; it was scooted back from the table and set at an angle. When asked why he positioned himself that way, he said he didn't like people at either end to look directly at him, so he'd move his chair—his body—to avoid eye contact in meetings. He sat at an angle for a similar reason, to avoid being directly across from anyone who could look right at him.
>
> It appeared that by moving himself away from his colleagues, Jack had put himself into a figurative corner.

The reason people never let Jack talk in meetings most likely had nothing to do with what he was trying to say, but instead how he used his body and eyes to communicate, or, in this case, *not* communicate, with others.

In practicing what felt comfortable to Jack—keeping his body separated from others and avoiding eye contact—he had physically communicated, albeit unintentionally, that he was not interested in his colleagues or, at the very least, he had nothing to say. Because what was doing was an accident, it is what is called "sending a miscue."

Our bodies are more important to the communication process than we realize, even when sitting around a table. Let's start by analyzing how our bodies help us to establish and maintain communication. Keep in mind that much of the time we communicate we are not seated around a table but we are walking, standing or multitasking.

Our Bodies Convey How Comfortable We Feel
We figure out people's intentions through their bodies just as much as we interpret what they say from their words. Language allows us to share information directly, but our bodies play a huge role in keeping everyone comfortable during the process. People who are comfortable are more receptive to what we are saying.

Observe how you feel with a person who looks relaxed, appears to be an engaged listener and is standing or sitting at the appropriate distance. These aspects of communication put others at ease, yet, until you are with someone who is unable to do these things correctly, you probably don't notice how they contribute to successful interactions.

You may send physical miscues when your body is a few inches too far away or a few inches too close; your head, shoulders and sometimes hips are turned away (even slightly); or your arms or neck appear stiff. *Any or all of these factors may make it uncomfortable for others to communicate with you,* even if you perceive yourself as friendly. When people feel uncomfortable around someone, they have a natural desire to get away from that person. And that's critical to know, because people have to feel comfortable before they want to keep interacting.

Most people intuitively learn how to convey comfort with their bodies. But some of us are not wired to do so. It's a learning weakness, but it is not typically identified as such in childhood and thus can easily continue unrecognized into our adult years.

With practice, you can learn to communicate more effectively with your body and relay a more positive message. The physical expectations of communication can be broken down into the following general areas.

The Physical Approach

As in all matters of communication, nuance is involved in how you approach people to talk with them, as well as how you exit from the interaction.

When you enter a group to participate in a conversation you come in *as a nobody to become a somebody*. Your entrance should be quiet, and your first goal should be to blend in. You shouldn't march in or burst into a group; instead make a subtle appearance. Nor should you enter a group and begin talking right away, even with close coworkers or friends. If you overhear the conversation, you still should come in as a listener. And when you talk, don't immediately start sharing your agenda; comment on what the other people are saying. Walking up too quickly to a group of people, speaking too soon or jumping in with your own ideas all can be seen as barging in or being disruptive, and it will give the impression that you think your contributions are more important than those of others.

Keep in mind that your physical approach turns on the social radar system of the group's members. They consider and try to determine your intent—whether you want to interact, ask a question, just hang out, or other possibilities.

As you approach people, they grow increasingly aware of your physical presence, and their brain sends a signal that tells them to shift their bodies to accommodate you. If you come into the group with your feet, hips and shoulders angled toward the people in the group, you've made a good start.

Your approach will depend on the situation. If it's one person standing alone, you come up with your feet, hips and shoulders opposite his or hers. When approaching a group of people who are standing and observing something together, you join the general line of the group so you can observe as well.

It is also possible to approach a group but not fully enter it in order to talk to one specific person briefly. To make this happen, you turn your body and your gaze more deliberately toward the person, and you stand outside the perimeter of the group by a foot or two. The person you approach will be trying to figure out why you are there and will react accordingly.

> Elise needed to ask her coworker Jill a question and saw her standing with others by the coffee machine. Elise approached the area where Jill was standing but did not enter the group. Instead, she stood a foot outside the group, angled toward Jill. This was enough to alert Jill, who now presumed from Elise's physical positioning that she had a quick question or comment, so Jill turned her shoulders and hips toward Elise to ask what she needed. Elise got her answer and walked away. Jill moved her shoulders and hips back toward the others and was reabsorbed into the group discussion.

Some folks don't know how to enter a group, nor do they know how to do a quick lateral approach to get a simple question answered or deliver a message. This can lead to feelings of isolation at work and thwart their efforts to do a good job.

The One-Arm Rule
The normal distance between two people who are communicating is one arm's length (this is in the United States; the rules vary by culture). This basic precept in communication, the *one-arm rule*, means that when you are talking to someone, you naturally stand about an arm's length away. The space in between is also known as *personal space*. If you stand too closely to someone (unless it's to establish intimacy), you may be causing that person to have uncomfortable thoughts and feelings. If you stand too far, you're communicating that you don't want to talk.

People with social anxiety or social processing difficulties have trouble maintaining what others feel is a comfortable distance. Some stand too far away or never enter a group, or they choose to observe from a short distance.

> Jason would stand by himself about six feet from a group and think about what he knew about the people. He wanted to be part of the group, but he expected everyone to come to him. He grew

increasingly agitated when his coworkers didn't seem to notice or care about him. We defined the hidden rule and asked him to think about it: "Groups don't go to people, it is expected that people go to groups." We also explained that he might have been perceived as unfriendly because he never approached the group and often looked upset. We worked with Jason on how to enter and exit groups, which helped him stay calm and get his social needs met.

* * *

Pam would approach a small group of people she considered her friends, but she often stood about four inches farther back than everyone else. While four inches doesn't sound like much space, it was enough to cause her peers to misinterpret her intentions. Pam believed she was still showing signs of friendship, but others interpreted her distance to mean that she was not comfortable with them, or not comfortable with herself. As a result, people were not very friendly to her. Although Pam said that her anxiety affected her confidence when entering a group, she still was not able to establish a strong physical presence, and therefore was not as socially successful as she would have liked.

Physical Distancing

If you aren't used to standing the customary arm's length from someone you're speaking with, you may have to retrain your brain's communication comfort zone. Simply knowing you should be an arm's length away is not enough; you have to practice the behavior to get comfortable with it.

Here are some things to notice that might indicate you have challenges with this particular skill:

- Do you stand closer than one arm's length, and do most people you speak to take a small step backward to try and establish their comfort zone?

- Do you stand farther than one arm's length in a group and find many of your comments quickly dismissed or even ignored?
- Do people frequently make their exit soon after you join the group?
- Do you stand too far away and do people not acknowledge or talk to you at all?

A common way to communicate that you want to leave a conversation is by slowly taking a small step backward. Distancing yourself physically is usually how you indicate you need to end the communication. Often this is accompanied by a brief, polite exit line like "See you later" or "Gotta get back to work, nice talking to you." You don't just abruptly turn and walk away.

Don't Forget About Those Feet, Hips and Shoulders
The one-arm rule is useful, but is only one aspect of physical presence to consider. Observe the sometimes small but significant differences in how nonverbal cues or body language communicates intent:

- It doesn't take much to send a nonverbal signal that you don't want to be with someone. A person standing at one-arm's length but with his feet, hips, trunk and head turned slightly away sends a signal that he has little desire to communicate. A person who stands like this may in fact be reacting to his own social discomfort (shyness or social anxiety), but his physical presence still makes others uncomfortable.

- A person who stands at an arm's length and with feet, hips, shoulders and head facing directly toward a group standing together, even if the people are just hanging out and not saying much of anything, indicates a clear desire to be included.

- A person facing a group who then turns his body away

at an angle sends a signal that he wants to exit the group. Others who notice this may stop including him in the conversation or talking to him altogether.

- Every set of rules has exceptions. When we want to communicate briefly with someone specific, it is common to disregard the one-arm rule and simply "pop" into a group. Standing a few feet away with our bodies angled toward the person, we say something like, "Are you busy after work?" We await the quick reply and then move on. In this situation, the question can be interpreted to mean, "Do you want to do something with me later?" The same words, however, might be interpreted differently if we ask the question more casually during the course of the day. "What are you doing after work?" in this case can be seen as polite chatter and not an invitation to go out later.

Our Body Movements are Part of the Process, Too

We are in nearly constant motion, even while talking. When we listen to someone speak, we are expected to gently nod our heads in agreement, using facial expressions to show that we are following along, changing the position of our arms and shifting our weight, all the while appearing at ease.

When we speak, our facial expressions are expected to match the tone of our message, and our body movements are supposed to communicate what we are feeling as well. This includes our shoulders, neck, head, hands, arms and hips.

If this sounds like an exaggeration, try standing stiffly while talking to someone, and you quickly realize how much our movements send messages and serve to keep others comfortable. Even seated, if people barely move and have rigid posture, we perceive them as less friendly and maybe so formal that we can't relate to them.

The level of ease with which we move our bodies at meetings, in conversational work groups or talking one-on-one can add to, or detract from the comfort level we bring to our communications.

Jane was a young adult who carried herself with great restraint. She sat, walked and stood stiffly. To her teachers she looked very alert, with perfect posture and her nose angled slightly upward. To her peers she seemed uptight, rigid, disconnected. Jane thought she looked like a good listener and had no idea others were perceiving her in a negative way.

When she came to our clinic, we role-played different sitting and standing postures, including a very stiff one resembling Jane's own. She accurately interpreted our postures, recognizing which ones made her feel comfortable and which did not. Once she understood how her posture was influencing the way people felt about her, she was very motivated to change. But it wasn't easy—her brain had practiced the stiff posture for over twenty years.

We began adjusting her sitting posture by having her slide her bottom forward a couple of inches in the chair, which automatically helped her shoulders to drop and her head to look more relaxed. Next, we asked her to shift her weight back and forth on her hips to relax the rest of her body. This proved to be especially challenging. So we got creative and encouraged her to watch the TV show Ellen, in which each episode kicks off with the audience and star Ellen DeGeneres dancing together.

Jane quickly zeroed in on how much audience members relaxed when they danced together as a group. Jane began to dance along at home—she had never danced before! She learned how it felt to shift her weight on her hips, and with practice she also learned how to engage her arms, hands, feet, head and neck. Once Jane became familiar with how it felt to move her body, we adjusted the movements to make them smaller. Today Jane may still not be the coolest person in the room, but she looks more relaxed than her previous self, making it easier for others to communicate comfortably with her. This process is ongoing; Jane's brain doesn't make it easy for her body to relax. But she gets why it's worth the effort.

THE THIRD STEP:
Use Your Eyes to Think About People as You Relate to Them

Our eyes are pretty powerful. That's why they're known as the "window into our souls."

Given this power, we use our eyes carefully in communications. They convey a lot of information about our thoughts and emotions, and we are constantly using our eyes to show we are thinking about the other person.

> Gary struggled socially all his life, but he couldn't quite put his finger on what was difficult for him. He was great at meeting smart women through an online dating service, and he set up interesting first dates, taking women to museums, picnics and the like. While the women seemed to enjoy themselves, few wanted to go on a second date. Gary decided to solicit their feedback to better understand what he was doing wrong. In their e-mailed responses, many commented on the "great date and good conversation"; some mentioned that they wanted to continue to be friends but they just didn't want to date him. These women were fairly consistent in their appraisal that Gary did something with his eyes that made them uncomfortable.
>
> Gary came to the ofiice so that we could better explore what he might be doing with his eyes. When he came in, he was friendly and relaxed. He sat

back in his chair, we conversed and he seemed fine. After fifteen minutes, I said, "I don't see what those women were seeing on your dates." He responded, "Oh, you want to see what I look like on a date?" He sat up straighter in the chair, turned one shoulder toward me, moved his head forward, leaned in and stared directly into my eyes.

"Got it," I said. "You are too intense."

Gary's understanding was that women wanted to feel as if their partners were giving them undivided attention, so he looked directly at his dates to show he was focused on them. He also had learned in a yoga class to concentrate by holding his body still. I explained that those behaviors might make a woman uncomfortable because she would feel he was thinking about her too intensely. We discussed how the rules of communication are not black-and-white but are more nuanced.

These insights became evident to Gary a few months later, after he had begun dating a woman more seriously. She complained that he was somewhat rude in public. To get a waiter's attention he would call out, and this upset his girlfriend. I explained that this likely had to do with how he was not thinking with his eyes. He now understood that he wasn't supposed to stare at women on a date, but he didn't know that he was supposed to stare at waiters to get their attention. Gary, an intrepid soul who always was willing to practice new skills, did not want to be perceived as rude, and he agreed to try thinking with his eyes by looking at a waiter to get his attention and not calling out to him.

The next week Gary e-mailed that he had initially believed thinking with your eyes was a bunch of nonsense, but he had tried it anyway. He was at a restaurant and was thirsty. Rather than holler to the waiter, he put his hand on his water glass and looked directly at the waiter—and remarkably the waiter came right over. Gary tried this again at a bar, not calling out his order but looking right at the bartender. He told me later, "I was never served so quickly before!"

Directed eye gaze is our strongest nonverbal signal that indicates that we want to interact. You may approach someone using the one-arm rule and establish a physical presence, but your intentions usually are not verified until you establish eye contact. It is only after you have approached people that you slowly turn your gaze toward their eyes or face (this also includes someone you know well, such as a spouse or friend). The eyes are like a *laser beam lock-on*. When the eyes connect with others, they convey clearly the intent and desire to communicate.

In fact, if you start talking before you look at someone, it can be confusing. The other person may wonder, "Is she talking to me? Why is she looking over there? Am I supposed to look where she's looking?" If you enter into a person's space and then fail to establish even brief eye contact, he is left wondering why you are really there.

Just as establishing eye contact is essential for conveying your intentions or desire to interact, too much direct eye contact can be interpreted the wrong way. If you see someone in a group across the room and stare directly at his eyes continuously as you approach, it will appear that you are trying to control—or steal—his attention.

In the work setting, however, it is appropriate to approach someone with the power of directed eye gaze when you have to communicate an important but quick message. It is totally acceptable to walk up and look directly at a person, whether he's talking to others or standing alone, to deliver an urgent message. Directed and constant eye gaze as you physically approach someone conveys a sense of urgency.

How Much Eye Contact is the Right Amount?

What people are looking at often reveals what they are thinking about, and can be a potent indicator of what they may be willing to talk about. So as you establish physical presence and stand with someone, you follow the person's eyes to discern what he or she is seeing, giving you information that you can then use in your conversation or just retain for informational purposes. Not noticing what someone is looking at can disrupt the flow of communication.

While this process is commonly described as using appropriate eye contact, we teach our clients that they are really *thinking with their eyes*. This is an important but subtle distinction. Using our eyes to initiate and maintain communication is about more than just looking. It involves *thinking* or *social thinking*—thinking about what others are feeling and thinking by picking up on their nonverbal cues. The ability to observe what someone else is looking at starts very young in life. Known as *joint attention*, it helps us to predict what others are thinking about.

The intensity of eye contact depends on a number of factors—how many people are in the group, whether your role is that of a speaker or listener (in formal and informal settings) and whether it is a particular kind of communication, such as one of intimacy.

As the speaker in a casual exchange (a conversation), you can look around a bit or briefly look up toward the ceiling as you get your thoughts together and consider what you're about to say.

As the listener in a casual exchange, you are expected to look toward the person who is speaking much of the time. But don't stare. You should monitor facial expressions and gestures to fully comprehend what the speaker is saying or trying to communicate. You can also look around briefly, as long as your gaze remains in the speaker's general direction. (Few of us can sustain full attention every second that someone is talking.)

As the speaker, you are permitted to look away briefly to keep your thoughts organized, but you're still expected to "check in" visually with the listener from time to time or at natural end points to send a message that *this information is for you*. Otherwise, the listener starts to feel that you are more interested in the sound of your own voice than in a personal connection. In this case, a listener might try and end the conversation by taking a step back and coming up with an excuse to leave.

We adjust our communication based on what we see in people's eyes and what we believe they are thinking and feeling based on the cues they're giving. For example, if you are speaking, and a listener looks confused, you are supposed to notice and adjust your language to clarify. Or if a listener appears distracted, you may try to figure out why and attempt to bring that person's attention back.

All of these hidden rules and nuances can be daunting to anyone. But if your brain cannot multitask in communication and you do best with words, you may struggle to pay attention to and understand all the nonverbal cues. You may have difficulty noticing and processing everything at once—facial expressions, the words being spoken, tone of voice, breathing patterns—and these all contribute to the overall meaning of what others are communicating.

In these cases, a communicative exchange can be an overwhelming experience that is ultimately more exhausting than it is informative. If you aren't able to pick up on all of the communication signals, you may not always understand what someone is trying to say and insist on a literal interpretation—even if the words do not match the facial expression, or they indicate the opposite meaning. For example, a colleague finds out the project he was working on has been canceled and comments sarcastically, "Oh, that's just *great*," though his eyes are downcast and his face shows utter disappointment; you might interpret his words literally and believe that he is glad and relieved rather than frustrated. Far more than most people realize, the eyes help us to understand what is being said.

Gary had strong technical work skills but some weak social skills, and he complained that people were getting frustrated with him at work. When he went to colleagues' offices to discuss projects, he would enter and ask if it was a good time to talk. Often they looked busy and would say, "No, this isn't a good time, but what do you want?" The ensuing conversations, he noted, often ended badly. He wanted to know what he was doing wrong.

I encouraged him to think about what he was doing with his eyes. Usually you don't just enter into people's space; instead you look to see if they notice you approaching. If they don't notice, and they appear to be involved in something else—working on the computer or packing up to leave work—you should consider postponing the conversation to another time.

Gary was planning to be more observant and think with his eyes, but he was concerned that he would startle people if he simply appeared in their doorway. So he decided he would also make a small noise as he approached, like rattling a piece of paper or clearing his throat. He sent the following e-mail to describe his experience trying this with two coworkers:

"As you recall, I was planning to get people's attention by making a little noise. The first person I tried it on is deaf in one ear and has partial hearing in the other. Much to my surprise, as soon as I appeared in her doorway, she looked up. We had a brief conversation about the visit she just made to her son at college—It went well. The second person I tried it on has full hearing and immediately looked up when I stood in his doorway. Maybe the noise isn't even necessary. Maybe all I need to do is appear at the edge of someone's vision, and if they're available, they will see me. I will experiment more with it when I have the next opportunity, which will probably be tomorrow morning. Tomorrow I will try it without noise and see if that works."

Gary sent this follow-up e-mail: "I've never thought about this at this level prior to working with you. The eye contact thing wouldn't have occurred to me if it had not been for you and my girlfriend. Thank you. Lots of growth and lots of work these days."

Those who find eye contact difficult or too intense may have developed strategies for avoiding it when speaking to others, not realizing that they may be sending a miscue that they don't want to be part of the interaction. A lack of eye contact can be interpreted as disinterest or even anger.

In some instances, differences in how one sustains eye contact can be cultural and unrelated to poor communication. Many Asian and American Indian cultures teach their children that it is a sign of respect to avoid eye contact with adults when they are communicating directly. However, in the United States and most Western cultures, avoiding eye contact shows a *lack* of respect. So while all of us are expected to *think with our eyes*, how and what we communicate are culturally determined social skills. Cultural sensitivity is an important consideration when interpreting someone's use of eye contact.

Tim was a senior in high school about to head off to study engineering at a top university, and he was attending a group through our clinic to practice social communication skills. One day when the guys in the group were conversing, Tim announced he didn't like to have to look at people while they spoke and would instead look at the floor, and he instructed the others to go ahead and talk to him anyway. We told him that even though he had shared his reasons, we, his communicative partners,

A FEW STRATEGIES FOR THOSE WHO HAVE TROUBLE CONNECTING WITH THEIR EYES

1. If you aren't using eye contact because you feel as if people are staring at you, know that they're probably trying to figure out if you're interested in communicating with them.

2. If you feel overwhelmed by eye contact, you can look toward someone's brow and cheekbones and still be perceived as looking at the person. At the same time, you need to explore what you can learn about others by thinking with your eyes. While this may start as an uneasy sensory experience, with practice you will become more comfortable with your eyes playing an active (and mandatory) role in communicative exchanges.

3. If the entire package of processing facial expressions and words is difficult, try pulling these apart to work on them. Many web sites show different facial expressions, which you can study without the interference of language. This is one way to help retrain the brain. You can also watch movies or TV shows with the sound turned off and follow the interactions more closely without relying on language to interpret scenes.

4. Using your eyes is critical to transmitting and receiving the entire message, and it helps people relate emotionally to you, and you to them. Avoiding eye contact because it is easier than doing it will cause others to disconnect emotionally from you.

felt emotionally that he didn't want to be with us, and we'd have a harder time including him in the discussion. People often adjust their behavior based on how others make them feel.

The normal social expectation is that we look toward people we're talking to, not just to maintain eye contact but to read and provide cues, to follow their train of thought and to connect emotionally. The more they genuinely seem interested in us, the better we feel about them. The concept of *thinking with our eyes* is a major factor in making that connection.

A Word on Eye Contact and Intimacy: Being Friendly, or Stalking Someone?

Look into the eyes of a spouse, partner, boyfriend or girlfriend and see how long it takes before it turns from a casual look into an unsettling stare. You should notice that this happens quickly, within seconds.

People use their eyes to capture someone's attention. In a meeting, when you want to make a point, you look directly at the people you're addressing. But if you're simply seated directly across from someone and you look at him continuously, that's staring.

Conversely, if you look away from that same person and never catch his gaze, it could be perceived as avoidance. And if you're speaking and don't establish eye contact once you finish, people may get the idea that what you said was dishonest or that you lack confidence in your message.

Staring or long looks can be interpreted different ways by different people. What one person sees as flirtatious interest another might perceive as creepy or stalking behavior even though these interpretations may be based more on perception than reality. It doesn't matter if your intent is to be friendly or show interest; you need to be aware of how others could perceive it.

THE FOURTH STEP:
Use Your Words to Relate to People When You Talk to Them

Language is important and definitely the most complex aspect of communication. However, it is one of many factors that influence the perception of effective communication. After the first three steps of communication—thinking about what we know about the other person, establishing physical presence and using our eyes to interpret and respond to the interaction—our language helps connect our thoughts to those around us.

> Ben talked a lot. He enjoyed being with people and sharing his ideas. He had much to say but few people who wanted to listen. Ben talked almost exclusively about himself—his thoughts, his experiences, his frustrations and his anger. The bottom line was that Ben was not able to make people want to listen to him. In fact, Ben's verbosity irritated others more than it ingratiated them; some he made furious. He was confused over why people avoided him and seemed angry, even though he worked so hard at his job. His perception was that he was friendly. Others saw him as annoying. Ben talked, but Ben was not an effective communicator.

A recurring message in this book is that we humans are pretty egocentric. That's why we choose to relate to the people who make us feel good about ourselves. How we respond to others is based on how we feel they've responded to us. So if we think someone has ignored us or treated us badly, we probably won't interact with that person in the future. We all constantly crave positive attention from others and hope they will find our minds interesting.

We learn a lot about what people think by listening to what they tell us about themselves, and how they show interest in us. Language creates the bridge to learning about each other, but when used poorly or insensitively it can also create a great divide.

The language game is very subtle. We use words to show that we are interested in other people's thoughts, opinions and feelings, even if we disagree with them or are actually not very interested in what they have to say.

> Scott was a professional working in the Midwest who allocated resources to develop programs in school systems. He selected nine schools (out of thirteen applicants) to receive funding for a special program. Shortly after the programs were up and running, Tracey, a representative of one of the funded schools, began to complain about weaknesses created by financial constraints in the program.
>
> Now Scott had a choice:
>
> First Scenario: He could simply tell Tracey what he was thinking by saying, "Tracey, if you aren't happy with the program, we can certainly give the money to one of the other schools that wanted it."
>
> Second Scenario: He could think about it from Tracey's point of view and respond, "I understand you are frustrated that there is not enough money to allow us to do all the things we want to in this program. I'm frustrated, too. Please consider if you can make a go of the program with its current allotment of funds. If not, let me know, and I'll see if one of the other schools is still interested in developing this program at its facility."

In the first scenario, Scott gets right to the point and tells Tracey what he is thinking. He's very efficient, but it doesn't make Tracey feel as if her thoughts are valued. While many of us would like to just get to the point, being blunt makes others feel less valued. When people don't feel valued, they start to complain, to each other and sometimes to their supervisors. In the first example, Tracey probably won't tell Scott how she feels about his bluntness, but she will go tell some of her closest coworkers about Scott's perceived insensitivity.

The second scenario takes a bit more time but is a more sensitive response. By first supporting how Tracey feels, Scott recognizes her feelings and connects them to his own, even though it leads to the same conclusion (letting her know that some other school would want the program).

Even though Scott may not relate to Tracey's emotions and more likely believes her complaints show a lack of appreciation, he is using a common strategy by recognizing and acknowledging her feelings. "I understand you are frustrated" is worth saying, even if it is not the complete truth, because it helps Tracey to feel understood.

We all say things we don't think are true. Scott may not feel for Tracey and may think of her as a whiner, but telling her he sees her point of view makes her feel valued. Managers are responsible for making workers feel supported, which gives them the sense they are on the same team.

If Scott told Tracey, "You're acting spoiled! Appreciate what you've been given!" he probably wouldn't last long at his job. Those in leadership positions have to manage employees' emotions as much as they manage their tasks and workflow.

Scott did a phenomenal job of getting funding to the schools, but it didn't end there; his success was also related to how his coworkers felt about him. Job success is based on many factors, but we are considered to be good employees when our fellow workers feel we are treating them with respect.

We Use Our Language Skills in Different Ways to Connect to People

Our language basically consists of questions and comments. That's it. The ratio of comments to questions appears to be about two-to-one. However, there isn't just one type of question or a single kind of comment. Here we will review different language strategies used to connect with people. To be comfortable communicators, we need to be versed in all the different ways people use language.

One trick to social language is to act as though we're interested in others. That's how we keep them showing interest in *us*. We try to connect emotionally to people, even if we're not all that keen on what they are saying. For example, your coworker may tell you about her new computer, which may be of little consequence to you and isn't important to your job. However, you can act interested, not only to make your colleague feel good but also because you can connect with her on some level about your own experience setting up or dealing with a new computer.

Connecting experience in this way helps people to bond emotionally, making for better teamwork and possibly friendship. Much of the workday is spent relating to each other socially and emotionally, and social conversations can lead to healthy networking. The social world and the work world are inseparable.

You should strive for balance in your communication skills. Monitor your language strategies, and if you notice that you rely on just one or two, you may want to practice adding different types of questions and comments to your interactions.

BASIC TYPES OF QUESTIONS
Baiting questions

These are questions we ask to get people to talk about what is interesting to us. If you're thinking about an upcoming trip, you may ask, "Are you going on vacation this spring?" Once they answer and you have responded to them about their comments, you have an opportunity to talk about your plans. By asking the baiting question, you successfully appear to be interested in the person, even though your true intent is to set up an opportunity to add your own thoughts on the topic. However, this doesn't mean you then take over or monopolize the conversation; there still needs to be social reciprocity. They talk, you listen and then respond to what they have said; then you comment, they listen and then respond to what you have said, and so on.

Personal questions
We think about what we know or remember about people before we begin talking to them. As we recall information, we'll ask questions that show what we remember. This is usually perceived as a compliment (as long as you don't recall memories that would embarrass people or seem like you're spying). If you remember that a colleague enjoys bike rides, you can ask, "Have you gone on any good bike rides lately?" As banal as this kind of question sounds, it shows you're thinking about the person.

Affirmation questions
These are questions we ask to show we're paying attention. This type of question is often rhetorical or more like a comment, for example, "Really, you said that?"

BASIC TYPES OF COMMENTS
Supporting comments
These are comments we make to support what people are saying. They can be short, one-word acknowledgements; for example, nodding your head and saying "Oh" or "Cool" or "Bummer" to show you're actively listening and supporting what the speaker is saying.

Supporting comments can also be longer and can show empathy by sharing your own experience without trying to make the conversation be about you. If a colleague is saying, "I had a really tough meeting with Mike," a supporting comment to show empathy and connect with the person would be, "I hate those meetings, I've been through too many myself. What happened?" In this situation, it would be considered insensitive or pushy to start talking at length about your own experience, unless you are specifically asked to elaborate, since it is your colleague who is upset and your attention should be focused on your colleague's need to vent.

Add-a-thought comments
These comments show we are connecting our experiences with the speaker's by weaving our life into theirs. This is likely the most common type of comment in any conversation. What's interesting about add-a-thoughts is they demonstrate that we don't really maintain a topic socially as much as we maintain a *connection* to the topic.

Look at the following examples of add-a-thought comments and you'll see that the starting topic was about taking the kids to soccer and working on the car, but the ending topic was house remodeling. When people connect to each other's experiences, they feel they've made a better emotional connection, and this is at the heart of human relationships.

To add your own thoughts, you listen to the speaker, think of connections to your own experiences, and then explain or support those connections. Notice in the following conversation how many different thoughts are woven together, but each one connects to a previous statement. No single topic is maintained, but the conversation is still successful.

- I say, "This weekend we have to take the kids to soccer, and then I hope to get some time to work on my car."

- A reasonable add-a-thought from you would be, "My car constantly breaks down. We're thinking of buying a new one."

- Then I might say, "We've been looking at buying a Toyota Prius."

- You can then connect to the environmental theme by saying, "Those are great cars. We're thinking about getting solar panels put on the house."

- I might then say, "We plan to do some remodeling on our house this summer."

- In which case you might say, "I never have time to work on my house. Work has been crazy lately."

A Few Words on Topic Starters for Conversations

In all but the most structured of meetings, we typically socialize or converse before working side by side with someone on a project. For some folks, figuring out how to start that social interaction can be the hardest part of the workday.

Many people over think conversations, expecting that they should all be intellectual or important. If you're one of those people, observe a routine conversation around the lunch table and you'll notice that it is not necessarily filled with wisdom and insight. Instead, most conversations are made up of comments that others can relate to. They allow us to share our thoughts and our emotional experiences, no matter how mundane.

Talking about what the local basketball team is doing or which stores are having sales, although not intellectually driven topics, brings people together by sharing observations and interests. We feel good about the people to whom we feel connected. If you don't participate in chitchat, you're often left out of the social mechanisms of the work environment. You may think this type of language exchange is a waste of time, but it actually encourages teamwork and the building of networks.

No one would say it's a waste of time to let children play, and we know it serves them well in many ways. Think of conversations as the adult form of play. If you need practice, start with small talk.

Here are some suggested topics for initiating a conversation:

SHARED MEMORIES: You can start a conversation about an experience you shared with someone by remembering a moment that was enjoyable or funny. Or you can comment on something you might have in common, a similar life experience you share. For example, "I hear you've worked in Silicon Valley for a long time. Where else have you worked?"

SEASONAL TOPICS: Events related to the calendar, such as holidays, weather or vacations, are frequent topic starters. Specific examples of seasonal topics include summer vacation, Thanksgiving, winter holiday activities, the Super Bowl, the Academy Awards, Memorial Day or Fourth of July plans. As you have likely noticed, the weather is a consistent topic for conversation. You can go anywhere in the world and you will find people talking about the weather. Why? It is the one thing everyone shares, regardless of culture, intellect or interests. Conversations are about sharing experiences, and since we all experience the weather together, it's easy to say what we think about it.

CURRENT EVENTS: Being aware of what is going on in the world helps to generate conversations, whether about news, cultural events, movies or other current topics. We frequently talk about happenings of interest in our communities, especially when we can reliably predict the reaction (say to a dramatic house fire or a politician accused of indiscretion). One note of caution here is to stay away from topics that fail to consider someone else's point of view. For example, boldly announcing your opinion on a political candidate can be controversial in a general office discussion but may be okay with a close group of friends. On the other hand, some topics are so far-reaching, such as world disasters that affect thousands of people or current events that are global in nature, that they are easy conversation starters.

OUR OBSERVATIONS OF THE WORLD: We observe people we pass on the street, or we notice how things seem to be going at work, and we make comments about what we see, hear or feel. While we always try to be sensitive not to offend or criticize, there is still a lot we observe that we can discuss and encourage others to comment on, even things we notice that are as banal as traffic patterns, empty storefronts or big sales.

In the next chapter we will explore in more detail how we use and interpret language. This is social algebra at its finest—figuring out what to say so we relate well to each other when the equation keeps changing. After all, aren't we all fairly complicated?

POINTS TO CONSIDER

❖ We try to connect emotionally to people, even if we're not all that keen on what they are saying.

❖ If you don't participate in chitchat, you're often left out of the social mechanisms of the work environment.

❖ Staring or long looks can be interpreted in different ways by different people. What one person sees as flirtatious interest another might perceive as creepy stalking.

❖ If you stand too close to someone, you may be creating uncomfortable thoughts. If you stand too far, you're communicating that you don't want to talk to that person.

❖ We adjust our communication based on what we see in people's eyes and what we believe they are thinking and feeling.

> "If everybody thought before they spoke,
> the silence would be deafening."
> ~ George Barzan

> "Two monologues do not make a dialogue."
> ~ Jeff Daly

Chapter 6

The Core of Communication
What People Mean by What They Say and How They Say It

"Choose your words carefully." We've all heard that expression, but what does it mean?

Language is a tool we use to share our thoughts and ideas, to relate, to commiserate, to argue and to explain. But language is more than just data to be fed in and then spit out; it is powerfully entwined with our emotions. This connection between language and emotions is part of every interaction, every day.

Even though we respond emotionally to what our coworkers say and do, we avoid speaking directly about the emotions themselves. When we get offended, we rarely discuss our feelings with the person who upset us; instead we will share our concerns with a manager or our colleagues. Complaining and gossiping is commonplace at work; telling coworkers directly that they made us feel bad is not.

Through clinical and field experience, and in conversations with supervisors after the fact, we have learned that people whose jobs are eliminated or who are fired because they irritated or annoyed others—due to social missteps—usually are not told the true reasons why they are being let go. Instead they're told it is for other reasons, or is related to the broad category of "job performance."

How Much Talking is Too Much . . . and What About Sticking to the Topic?

As adults, what we say and how we say it are evaluated at the level of nuance. Just as our emotions become compressed with age, so does our language. We are expected to say more with fewer words. It is important to understand this nuance, because it will increase your awareness of how others analyze and interpret your social behavior.

So how much do you say and when? Because the rules of communication shift based on the shifting expectations of each circumstance, figuring out how much information to share has to do with the situation and what you know about the people in the situation.

> Allan had never held onto a job for more than two years, and he contacted our clinic to ferret out the possible reasons. At the time, he was employed as a manager. After a number of coworkers told him he was annoying or bothersome, without ever explicitly saying why, Allan inferred that his problems at work stemmed from the challenges he had connecting socially with people.
>
> In the course of our e-mail exchanges, we noticed that Allan was redundant, starting a topic by explaining something he had already shared in a previous e-mail. When we pointed this out, he admitted that he often restated his thoughts or ideas because he assumed people would not understand or remember them otherwise. He said he did this not just in e-mails but also in conversations and meetings as well. We told Allan that people are expected to infer meaning and recall information from previ-

ous discussions or experiences. He agreed to be less repetitive in his communications and to try not to assume his colleagues didn't understand or recall what he'd told them. Until our e-mails shed light on his habit and how it affected others, Allan had been unaware how bothersome and offensive it was, because the behavior was at the level of nuance.

When you speak to people, they are pulling up prior knowledge about the topic and making inferences based on what they know about the world. If you tell a co-worker you are going to Hawaii for a meeting and then to vacation, he should be able to infer the following:

- You are going on a plane.
- You're bringing a bathing suit with you.
- You plan to relax in the sun and the water.
- You probably won't settle down in the hotel and work quite as hard as you do on other business trips.

Because it is assumed that most people have a basic understanding of how things work, it wouldn't be necessary for you to make all four points; instead you'd know that the person gets the gist of what you're saying. If he wants to talk to you about your trip, he'd ask questions to advance the conversation, such as "Which islands are you visiting?"

Any successful language-based exchange must have a point. When we read a book, we try to figure out or infer what the writer is saying before we get to the end of a section or chapter. In the same way, the listener tries to figure out the speaker's intentions before the speaker even finishes expressing the thought.

Allan lacked insight about how much others knew, and that's why he often said too much. Even those with insight might still decide to provide *color* or background by adding a lot of extra facts and details—but that also makes it hard to follow what it is they're trying to convey. At times others want to say and, in fact, *may* say, "Can you get to the point?"

The amount of time it takes to relay a message is an important component of successful communication. When someone gives too many basic details, or is tangential and not focused on a particular thought or idea, it can be frustrating to the listener. We speak to make a point, and we make sure to give others time to share their ideas as well. This mean monitoring how long we speak. Too long, and we can be seen as disrespectful or self-centered because we aren't allowing someone else an opportunity to talk.

There are no set rules for how long to talk, because it depends on the situation, but the following variables illustrate how much detail may be acceptable in conversation. We use different types of language for different situations.

GROUP MEETINGS: Typically in meetings people have come together for a specific reason, and the hidden rule is that you should make your comments short and to the point. Meetings usually are agenda-driven, and sticking to the agenda is critical. There are too many people listening to allow one person to wander around in his or her thoughts. This is not a time to review or restate all that you know about the agenda item. Any discussion should provide information that others likely have not thought about or do not already know. You also should assume that people have the same basic information that you do, even if they aren't saying it out loud. A productive meeting is one in which participants get the necessary information to move them forward and aren't hindered by one person speaking too long, stating the obvious or going off-topic, all of which drag out the meeting and leave others annoyed.

MEETINGS ATTENDED BY SOMEONE HIGH UP IN THE COMPANY HIERARCHY: The hidden rules of a routine work meeting change and require us to become more formal and attentive when the speakers are on the management or supervisory level (and not support staff). If you do need to speak, be brief and get to the point more quickly. Talk about ideas that the special person in attendance wants to hear about. The adjustment in the hidden rules does not minimize how individual employees are valued, but rather is meant to show respect for the particular time demands of the special attendee. The discussion is kept concise and at an appropriate level so the person can be spared from conversations and decisions that take place on a lower level. Those in higher levels of management usually don't want to know the specific details of a project; they just want to know about important developments, such as timelines and budgets.

> Jon, a sales associate, had been describing strategy at a meeting attended by a few managers and engineers. As soon as the company CEO walked in, the focus of the meeting shifted. Jon's manager took over, reporting on what Jon and members of his team were doing. Jon was dissuaded from making further comments. He left the meeting furious. He wanted to know why he was not permitted to speak and his manager was allowed to "look good," when a lot of the work he reported was based on Jon's contributions. We worked with Jon to recognize the hidden rules of meetings and how they shift based on what you know about the people in attendance. In this situation, the manager was expected to step in when the CEO was present. Jon perceived himself as a hard worker who didn't get enough recognition for his contributions, but others saw him as a difficult and contentious employee who failed to understand his role in the company.

INFORMAL WORK COMMUNICATIONS: Outside of meetings, communicating with a co-worker usually starts on a personal level with an initial greeting and eventually a brief comment or question. After that, however, we must share relevant information in a focused, succinct way, making sure to stick to the core topic. We listen carefully to the person's response to understand how he is interpreting what you have said and respond back conveying that you hear him and understand him, even if you don't agree with his ideas.

Work-based discussions are considered satisfying when we feel our ideas have been addressed and we have learned something of value from our workmate. Our emotional response is based on how we feel about the working relationship and whether we think we share the same goals, or we at least understand what we need to do to work well together. Our response also has to do with whether we feel the person appreciates our contribution and is not appearing to take credit for our work or the work of others.

SOCIAL CONVERSATIONS: Coworkers get together socially during breaks, at lunch, or after work to hang out. Work-based business exchanges are very different from social conversations, in that work exchanges are topic-driven while social conversations are more emotion-driven. Unlike meetings with specific agendas, people hang out socially to connect in a more casual way, with the basic underlying agreement that they will try to make others they are with feel good. Any topic has to be one that most people can relate to, such as sports teams, the weather, family, holidays or movies.

The connection to each topic is more relaxed in a social conversation, unlike a discussion at a work meeting where everyone is required to adhere to the agenda. So I might say, "Real estate prices are really good right now; we're thinking of buying a house." You might reply, "We've lived in our house for twenty years, I couldn't *think* of moving." And another person might say, "Our neighbors just got a new green kitchen installed," at which point the group may start talking about the benefits of green technology. Social conversations bend and flex according to our experiences. A conversation is satisfying if we feel that we are connecting emotionally with the other people in the group.

GETTING TO THE CORE OF COMMUNICATION: WE ARE ALL TRYING TO INTERPRET EACH OTHER

The human brain takes in information from many different

channels to get a clear picture of what someone means by what he or she says. The words alone represent only one aspect of what is being communicated. We listen to these words and then interpret them based on several factors.

THE SITUATION: A good book starts with a description of the setting. This writer provides this context to help the reader better understand the characters. In real-life communication, the setting similarly helps us understand the information and people within it. For example, if a coworker is packing up his bag to go home, it is a poor time for a long conversation about a work problem. That person has probably mentally called it quits for the day and will be unhappy about having to stay and deal with your problem. However, if the situation is a meeting that has been arranged specifically to talk about the problem, then this is the ideal setting to problem-solve. Reading the situation in this fashion helps us decide if it is a good time to talk to someone about a work-related issue.

WHAT YOU KNOW ABOUT THE PERSON: If you know someone to be rather unfriendly and always in a hurry, then you will want to get right to the point. However, if you know someone well and are on friendly terms, then getting right to the point and not acknowledging him personally may offend him or lead him to believe you are angry, because you are being too businesslike—paying more attention to the information than to the person.

WHAT IS SAID: Listen to the language spoken, but be careful not to take everything that is said literally. We have to interpret the language based on the considerations outlined here, including the particular situation and what we know about the person. We also have to regard *how* the words are said, which involves factors such as tone of voice and volume.

Many adults are overly literal. They get stuck thinking a phrase or word has one meaning, rather than interpreting the meaning by looking at everything that's happening at the time the words are spoken. Many people who are too literal understand that language can be figurative, and they can and do use idioms and metaphors successfully. But they run into trouble when it comes to understanding how the same sets of words can mean different things in different situations.

> Robyn, a professional woman in her thirties, prided herself on her vocabulary and sophisticated use of language. She was quick to note when others did not express themselves well. She also would make a point of telling people when they said something she believed to be wrong. If they defended their point of view, Robyn would correct them again. When she was told, as she often was, that she was being argumentative, she would insist that she was simply explaining. She felt dumbfounded that her intentions could be so misinterpreted.

TONE OF VOICE: Listen to the quality of the voice to help determine the meaning of the words. The voice can communicate alarm or be toned down slightly to indicate concern, depending on its pitch and volume. Tone of voice also can be used to turn what someone is saying into a question or a statement. Tone of voice, like emotions and language, also becomes compressed with age. Although a subtle shift to a higher tone or frequency may indicate excitement, we don't expect an adult and an eight-year-old to express excitement in the same way.

FACIAL EXPRESSION: Watch the face; it provides emotional information that tells how the person feels about what he is saying. This helps you to know whether he is being sarcastic, for example, or feeling upbeat or sad.

BODY LANGUAGE AND EYES: Note whether a person uses body language to help make his points more emphatically through gestures or eye contact.

THE PERSON'S MOTIVE: Why do you think the person is sharing this information with you? What point is he trying to make? Figuring this out is more complicated and may require evaluating all of the above factors, as well as other information specific to your workplace. Language is motive-driven, and understanding the motive—why someone is saying what he is saying—is an important step in interpreting it. Remember that at the same time we are trying to figure out the person's motives, he is trying to figure out ours. For example, if our motive is to share information on a topic but we end up talking for too long, this suggests that our motive is wanting to show off. Misinterpreting each other's motives is a frequent source of confusion and miscommunication.

Context is the set of information surrounding a situation; it is dynamic and requires us to process and respond to a lot of input simultaneously. And the context can change rapidly. We've all heard people complain that their words were misinterpreted or taken out of context. But context is not just one thing—it is many things happening at the same time.

If all of this feels overwhelming, start by focusing on each part. To retrain your brain, you have to break down and evaluate how you approach a situation using the parameters outlined above. (Refer to Chapter 5 for additional communication strategies.)

An interesting and entertaining way to explore these communication parameters is by watching the clay-animated TV show *Pingu* (available on YouTube). An anthropomorphic penguin family communicates through tone of voice and body language, with no words ever spoken. It is fascinating to observe how we can interpret the communication without any language being used.

What About Sarcasm? How Does That Work?
Not all communication can be taken at face value. Sometimes interpreting people's intentions means discerning when a message is being expressed through humor. Although humor is a way to communicate in a lighthearted fashion, often there is an underlying point being made.

Sarcasm requires more refined social interpretation. Slapstick humor is obviously silly—tripping over a board, falling down, walking into a wall. Sarcasm is subtle, bearing many of the features of predictable communication but with one or more aspects out of sync. If someone is discussing a project that is taking extra time and says in a flat, unexcited voice, "I can't *wait* to work all weekend on it!" you should interpret this as sarcasm, because at least one element of communication—tone of voice—does not match the words spoken.

Interpreting sarcasm requires social thinking, which starts with taking perspective and includes our own knowledge of how the world operates. In the example above, we know that very few people really want to work on the weekend when they have already worked Monday through Friday, so we can assume the comment is sarcastic.

Doing the social fake
Like humor, another form of communication that is not literal or entirely truthful is *the social fake.*

We're all encouraged to be honest from an early age, but telling the truth all of the time is socially quite problematic. The real truth? We don't always tell people exactly what we are thinking, especially when it can hurt or offend them. This goes for coworkers, friends and even life partners.

Most of us tell *white lies,* or harmless fibs, to protect others from our harsh thoughts. If someone asks, "What did you think of my report?" start with a positive response—"It made some good points." Even if you think the report has problems, don't begin with a criticism, because then the person probably will be unwilling to listen to your other thoughts, no matter how constructive. If an acquaintance asks, "How do you like my new shoes?" and you don't particularly like them, you might say, "Oh, where did you get them?" or "They look comfortable" to diffuse the question and move the conversation along. Or if you must, you could say they look nice or you like them even though they're not your favorite style. You're not really lying; you're helping the person to feel good about herself.

Remember, we feel good about the people to whom we feel emotionally connected. Most of us routinely tell others what we think they want to hear, and not necessarily our true or unfiltered thoughts, especially when the topic is of little consequence or our opinion isn't crucial. This is one way to maintain healthy work relationships, friendships and marriages—doing the social fake.

Carl was a graduate student participating in a social thinking group for young adults at our clinic. As we began to talk about the importance of the social fake, he became very serious and said earnestly, "What I have to say is important to me, so I want it to be important to others. I do not want to think anyone is faking interest in what I have to say; I want them to be genuinely interested in me!" As the session continued, another member of the group began to express her ideas. As soon as Sheryl began to speak, Carl looked away from her and began talking to himself. When we pointed out that he did not appear to be genuinely interested in what Sheryl had to say, and that furthermore his lack of attention would be seen as inconsiderate in the world outside of the clinic, he recognized his double standard and apologized.

Still, it is not easy for Carl to simply start "faking it." He needs to begin with an awareness of how he wants or expects others to behave when he is talking, and then he needs to behave similarly in return. This will keep people feeling good about him.

We are less than honest in our communication on other fronts. When we live with someone for a long time, we routinely ask the person, "How was your day?" We are asking not only to find out about our partner's day, but also to determine his or her mood and figure out the most peaceful way to share the evening hours together. If our partner had a bad day, it could signal irritability and it wouldn't be a good time to bring up a potentially difficult topic. By taking care of others' feelings, we are taking care of how they treat us in return, which means we are taking care of ourselves.

> Leon was a bright teenager stuck on the idea that he should always tell the truth no matter what. When told that at times a response is simply meant to take care of how people feel, he responded, "OK, I won't tell them the truth. But if someone asks me if she looks fat in an outfit, and I think she's fat, then I'll just say, 'You don't want to know the answer to that question, because it's so obvious.'" We pointed out why his suggested response would backfire because people interpret our language in part by interpreting our intentions. Leon's intention was to avoid saying outright that she was fat, but the person would easily be able to interpret that through his language, and she'd still feel hurt.

Being careful with our language to not cause people to feel bad is one of the keys to positive social communications. Taking care of people's feelings is usually more important than being truthful all of the time. It's what we expect from our friends, and it's what we do so others keep having positive thoughts about us.

Contentious Versus Supportive Relationships

We now know that part of social communication is figuring out people's intentions and anticipating their emotional reactions. This can get mighty confusing and present social challenges in the work world, where teamwork is often vital for a company's success. Combine a project deadline with a mandate to collaborate with colleagues, and at some point you will feel irritated or frustrated by a coworker who you think is getting in the way of your creativity or your ability to get work done.

Working well together through tense times is an important part of the work experience. How you handle it makes an important difference in how you are perceived. It's easy to be friendly and convivial when times are good, but figuring out how to be supportive of your colleagues during tough times may mean going the extra mile or stretching yourself socially.

> Hugh helped to maintain the library system for a school district in New Mexico. He did a great job of keeping the libraries running and training library aides to help at the branches during the school day. In general, Hugh related well to people when he felt calm and in control. During a routine visit to check in with an aide, he walked into the library to find the lights turned out and books scattered on the floor while students were present. He was really upset to see students exposed to unsafe conditions and immediately went to the aide to question her. He was hostile in his inquiry and let her know the situation was unacceptable.
>
> Although Hugh was absolutely correct that the library was unsafe and that the aide should have taken care of it, by immediately showing his anger he put the aide on the defensive. She felt embarrassed that he scolded her in front of students and was upset that he did not show respect for her feelings. She complained to Hugh's boss, and he called Hugh in to discuss his behavior.
>
> Hugh was confused. Wasn't it his job to keep the libraries maintained to serve the school community? Hadn't the aide let him down?

> Even though Hugh was right to be upset about the aide not doing her job (we all have pretty strong feelings at times), he erred in openly expressing his anger. He had limited awareness of how strongly work relationships are social relationships, and that we have to take care of people's emotions at work if we want cooperation. Had Hugh started by being supportive rather than contentious, he'd have had more success helping the aide problem-solve to do her job better. Instead, by showing his true feelings, he gave her the opportunity to vent emotionally to fellow coworkers and to his superiors.

Once an employee gets angry, a lot of work time is lost to his or her need to complain about the situation. In fact, research indicates that the quickest way to establish work friendships is by "bitching together." While this might make for lots of friends at work, it doesn't do much for productivity!

A friend of Hugh's offered this insight after hearing about his struggles: "There is more to a valued employee than just someone who can get the job done. Working well with others is a necessary job skill. If you're not doing it, it probably is grounds for firing—especially if your coworkers are feeling disrespected on a regular basis."

Now when Hugh sees an employee doing a less than adequate job, he might ask, "Is there anything I can help you with?" After offering ideas to make tasks easier, he can point out one or more of the person's strengths before launching into the larger matter at hand and proposing solutions. This kind of diplomacy is time-consuming, but in the long run it keeps things running smoothly and is a more effective way to communicate.

Across the workday we form social-emotional relationships, and they can easily make or break a job experience. Even if we have good credentials, a strong résumé and excellent technical experience, it still may not count for much if we don't make the people we work with feel valued. We may not lose our job, but we also may not get that promotion we thought we deserved, giving us one more reason to be frustrated with folks around us.

If you feel like you constantly have a reason to vent about how people at work mistreat you, it's a good idea to step back, evaluate how you might be seen through their eyes, and try making adjustments in your behavior. Many adults I've worked with conclude they aren't doing anything wrong; they say the problem is that they consistently work with difficult people—no matter where they work!

How do any of us survive the tumultuous waters of human relations, especially work relationships? We do it with nuance.

> Fred, a grocery store manager, thought he was being diplomatic with coworkers by telling them straight out that he didn't like their ideas, and then offering assurances that his opinion didn't change the way he felt about them personally. This tactic backfired for an obvious reason. People are connected emotionally to their ideas, so Fred was essentially saying, "I don't like this part of you."
>
> On the other hand, Patty had a gift for making people feel good even when she didn't agree with their ideas. One coworker recalled how Patty was so positive and nuanced in her comments, she managed to communicate an alternative point of view almost seamlessly. "Patty is so nice to work with!" he said. "I had an entire conversation with her, never felt threatened or put down when she told me to change my approach and now I think about the problem in an entirely different way."

**HERE ARE SOME TIPS
TO HELP YOU NOTICE IF YOU ARE CREATING
A CONTENTIOUS RELATIONSHIP**

- You hear through the grapevine or sense that someone is annoyed with you, but you assure yourself you are right and he is wrong.

- You spend much of your time explaining your point of view rather than soliciting his point of view; you spend more time talking than listening.

- When he tries to explain why you should consider his point of view, you become defensive and reiterate yours.

- You don't concede to making a mistake, even if it made him feel bad. Maybe you just want to move on, but he will retain strong memories of his negative emotions.

**HERE ARE SOME TIPS
ON DEVELOPING A SUPPORTIVE WORK RELATIONSHIP**

- When you feel annoyed with a coworker, push yourself to try and see things from his point of view.

- Acknowledge he has a different perspective and some good ideas.

- Accept the assumption that some of the project can be done incorporating his ideas.

- Spend time relating to him in a positive way, both about his work and his life outside of work. As you build trust, he will be more open to your opinions about work-related matters.

- Acknowledge that you may have upset him with a gentle apology: "Hey, I'm sorry for the way I acted. I was stressed out."

- Even if you feel his ideas are not valuable, you still let him know you value working together. In other words, you don't treat him according to what he is saying in any particular moment, and you don't judge him by a single idea.

INDIRECT COMMUNICATION: READING BETWEEN THE LINES

What is *not* said can be more powerful that what *is* said. How do we discern meaning from the silence?

> Bill was a talkative guy. So much so that he never seemed to stop talking. From Bill's point of view, he was communicating the only way he knew how. Bill was unaware how much communication has to do with inference, or "reading between the lines." He didn't know that he could communicate or imply a lot of information without directly stating it—that in fact there is plenty to infer from what isn't said.

People regularly use indirect communication, implying what they mean without directly stating it. Or, put another way, we interpret what people mean by what they *don't* say.

> Dakota was a relatively new hire, someone who had come to our clinic when he was a student. Smart and enthusiastic, he assisted in our company mailroom. We developed some new procedures to manage how books are mailed and asked our assistant Andrea to review these with Dakota. After explaining the new procedures, she asked Dakota, "Sound good?" This was a rhetorical question, but Dakota assumed it meant she was asking his opinion. He told her at length why he didn't think the procedures would work and said he preferred to use the old ones.

Andrea came back to our office and told us she couldn't work with Dakota because he was argumentative and disrespectful. A few days later, we met with Dakota and asked what he thought of the new procedures. He said initially he hadn't liked them, but now that he had tried them he saw the new way was better. When we told him he had upset Andrea, he denied that he had argued with her and said he simply had answered a direct question. Together we explored indirect language and discussed how people rarely tell you exactly what to do, and instead imply direction, as Andrea had. Dakota needed to work harder at figuring out or inferring people's intentions.

Review each of the following scenarios and think about how someone might interpret their meaning, especially when something is not directly stated.

INDIRECT STATEMENT/ACTION: You never ask for help, although people routinely ask you for help.
IMPLICATION: You don't think anyone you work with is worthy enough to help you.

INDIRECT STATEMENT/ACTION: You never greet people at the office.
IMPLICATION: You don't care about the people you work with; you are unfriendly.

INDIRECT STATEMENT/ACTION: You never acknowledge someone else's ideas as being good; you argue at meetings about how your ideas are better.
IMPLICATION: You think only your own ideas are good. You aren't considerate of others and lack the skills to work as part of a team.

INDIRECT STATEMENT/ACTION: You don't remember significant things people tell you about their lives.

IMPLICATION: You are self-focused on your work and accomplishments, and you minimize important aspects of your coworkers' lives.

INDIRECT STATEMENT/ACTION: You ask a person at work—someone of the opposite sex who also happens to be single—if she wants to have dinner with you.
IMPLICATION: She thinks you want to date her.

How your message is interpreted is often more important than what you intended to communicate.

> Forrest was a teacher who tried to bond with his teenage students by joking around with them. One day a female teacher walked into his classroom to ask a question about scheduling. Believing he was paying the teacher a compliment, Forrest announced in front of the students that she had a good body and told her she looked like Angelina Jolie. Forrest then pulled up a picture of the movie star on the Internet to show to the students. The teacher left the room upset and went to complain to the principal, and Forrest was put on probation for sexual harassment. Forrest could not understand how his comment could be interpreted as anything other than a lovely compliment. But no one else in the school where he taught perceived it that way; instead his comment was seen as degrading to the female teacher.

The following illustrations demonstrate that focusing on how we act and how we are perceived can impact us in a positive way. The "SEB-Path Options" (Social-Emotional-Behavioral Path Options) can help us to visualize how intertwined our social emotional behavior is in regard to how we are perceived and how our actions are interpreted by others. The situational outcomes differ depending on the behavioral-emotional path that is chosen and the social emotional chain effect that takes place due to our actions and the message we are sending to others. This tool can be used to highlight the importance of the social emotional connections that are made with each other. Even a seemingly simple scenario such as sharing an idea at work can have dramatically different results depending on the behavioral choices/pathways and emotional connections we make.

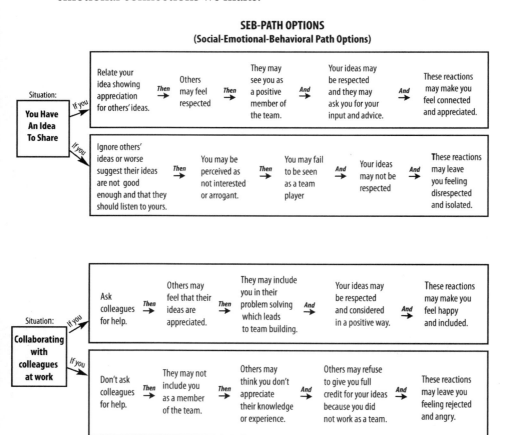

We spend much of our day trying to figure out other people. That is why we are constantly reading people—to understand their intentions, anticipate their emotional reactions and establish what it is they are trying to communicate by what they say, and what they don't say.

POINTS TO CONSIDER

- ❖ Taking care of people's feelings is usually more important than being truthful all of the time. It's what we expect from our friends, and it's what we do so others keep having positive thoughts about us.

- ❖ Even if you feel someone's ideas are not valuable, you still let the person know you value working together.

- ❖ We speak to make a point, and we make sure to give others time to share their ideas as well.

- ❖ Most of us tell "white lies," or harmless fibs, to protect others from our harsh thoughts.

> "The world is so wide and each of us so small —
> yet bound by friendship we are giants."
> ~ Pam Brown

> "The nice thing about teamwork is that you always
> have others on your side."
> ~ Margaret Carty

> "Coming together is a beginning, staying together is
> progress, and working together is success."
> ~ Henry Ford

Chapter 7

Fitting In
The Importance of Conformity, Teamwork and Networking

As we explored in the previous chapter, choosing the right words, not expressing certain thoughts out loud, or not being negative about ideas we don't necessarily find agreeable are some of the things we do to build up our social relationships and create an environment for successful teamwork and networking. The positive recognition that comes from all of this not only feels good, but is also attached to success and job security.

Sometimes though, despite our best and most diligent efforts, the personal and professional recognition we think we've earned or deserve just doesn't happen. The reasons why may be simpler than they seem.

ORMITY

mity a bad thing or a good thing or does it fall some-
e middle? It depends on how you look at it.

We come to any job with special talents, accomplishments and skills. Presumably we are hired because of those very abilities that define us as individuals. We all want to be noticed for the good things we do. But we are nearly always expected to contribute as part of a team. So how do we balance who we are—our uniqueness—with the expectations for success at work?

Here's the interesting thing. *Often we have to conform to the group's expectations in order to be celebrated as unique within the group.* If we don't conform, and we just stand out as different, we will not be considered strong members of the group, and as a result may have a much harder time getting our ideas heard and appreciated.

People working in groups form microsocieties. Social norms are established and participants are expected to interpret the norms so they can work together. Individual contributions are embraced, as long as the individuals have adhered to the social expectations of the group.

> We were giving a talk at a large bookstore, and there wasn't enough room for all attendees to sit in the provided chairs. Most of the latecomers had to sit or stand on the perimeter. All but one person managed to do so; this man was lying across the floor, as if in bed, while he listened to me speak. We couldn't help but have an uncomfortable thought about him. He seemed interested in listening to what we had to say, but he was not conforming to the norm of how everyone else listened to the presentation.
>
> At the end, he approached and told us that while he had enjoyed our talk, he thought we'd made it sound as if it were necessary for all people to conform to be part of a group. He was from Berkeley, California, he said, where residents were known for being nonconformists. While he spoke, we observed that he was shaved, appeared to be

attentive to his hygiene and had on an expensive suit—all signs of a certain level of conformity.

Conformity was evident even among the people perhaps best known for being nonconformists—the hippies in the 1960s and 1970s in the San Francisco Bay Area. They dressed alike, listened to the same music and used the same idioms. While they said they were not conforming, they in fact were defined by the expected norms and how they conformed as a social group, even if it was different from their parents' notions of conformity.

We all conform, more than we probably realize. Through conformity, we seek to be recognized for our individuality and uniqueness.

Starting in preschool, if we don't conform to group expectations, we can't learn as part of a group. Throughout our lives, we continue to conform—on our work teams, with our friends and our families—to make living easier for everyone. Conforming doesn't mean we let go of our ideas; it means we all agree to limit or manage how we say and do things according to the hidden rules or social expectations of the specific circumstance. Each of us will have unique thoughts, but we adjust how we frame our thoughts based on how we want to exist together—usually we are seeking harmony—with those around us. For example, we might refrain from stating an opinion in a way that it could offend someone in the group.

We act in a way that shows we understand what others expect, and that allows them to keep having normal or good thoughts about us. In contrast, when our behavior causes people to have uncomfortable thoughts about us, they may move away or exclude us. Remember, it is natural to seek out people who make us feel comfortable.

TEAMWORK

Many bright individuals with social learning challenges also have amazing, creative ideas to share. Unfortunately, they don't know how to get people to listen to them, so their ideas don't float. It takes intellectual drive to come up with good ideas, but it takes social thinking and related social skills to get others to listen to those ideas and work together.

Teamwork, negotiation, cooperation, respect—all are important social conformity concepts, meaning we may have to give up a bit of what we want to say or do in the moment in order to take care of someone else's thoughts and related feelings. This is what helps to maintain steady relationships.

In successful teamwork, people participate by sharing their imaginations. Each contribution becomes part of a collective pool of ideas, and in that way every person influences the team vision of the project. There is time for brainstorming, where all suggestions are considered; pruning, where the team narrows in on the leading proposals to go forward; and then moving on, where the group focuses on agreed-upon key concepts—and at this point, ideally, anyone whose ideas were rejected does not take it personally and lets go of negative emotions.

Taking time to listen to others' ideas—and figuring out what they mean by what they say—is part of teamwork. So is spending time helping a coworker with his or her idea, rather than focusing on making your own come to life.

An unspoken rule in teamwork says that if you help me out, I will help you out at some point down the line. "Helping out" does not have to mean literally giving help; instead it can mean I'll "watch your back," or stand up for you, at a time when you need an ally on the team. Also implicit in this agreement of trust is that by working together, we can create a better end result—better than if we worked separately on the same thing. That's what is behind the saying "Two heads are better than one."

Those of us not born with intuitive social thinking lack the natural ability to learn the interpersonal skills needed for this kind of teamwork. Practicing team skills is something that starts in preschool, but some of us missed out on practicing the nuances of social communication. As children we may have preferred isolated play, where we used our imagination to build or create by ourselves. During the school years, we likely did not engage much with peers, usually working alone and avoiding group study, even as we soared academically.

Then the time came to enter the workforce. In much of the work world, all are expected to function as a team, putting our minds together to conceptualize or build a product. Those of us with social weaknesses may be thoughtful and productive when it comes to our particular area of interest, but we may not be versed or well practiced in the subtle give-and-take of being a team player.

Although we may be able to understand others on an intellectual level, we need practice in our social thinking and related social skills. Many of us are fine in our first years on a job, when we are simply contributing to the team. But if we are recognized for our outstanding work or acuity and promoted to a higher position, the lack of practice in sophisticated team play becomes apparent. While we may be able to engage in basic teamwork, it becomes difficult to manage others effectively. In most companies, each promotion requires not only advanced knowledge or abilities, but a higher level of social and organizational skills as well. Thus, some who are considered good members of a team struggle tremendously in management positions.

> Lenny, a fifty-year-old with a master's degree from a well-known technical university, sought our services after being demoted from his position as a project manager. Humiliated, he expressed his concern about being able to keep his job, as he was now working and competing with "hot shots" fresh out of universities. Lenny was removed from the management position and restored to his old job because he could not keep an open mind to all the different needs of his team members, and he tended to focus too much on the one aspect of his team that he preferred—quality control.

In many people the social brain is highly flexible, able to adapt to a variety of situations and quickly access information needed to process each one and react accordingly. But not everyone has this social flexibility. Learning how to look beyond our own interests to those of the team is a challenge, but an important one to continue to work on and improve.

NETWORKING

Beyond teamwork are networks—not the popular online social networking sites but the traditional, time-honored practice of making and maintaining personal connections through face-to-face contact in the workplace. In this definition, a network is about developing work-based relationships and showing interest in each others' lives.

For example, asking a colleague during lunch or a midday break about her weekend demonstrates a regard for who she is outside of work. This kind of friendly chitchat indicates that we value this person as an individual, not just as a coworker.

There is no formula for how much time to spend on networking. It depends on the culture at each workplace. Networking happens throughout the day and on a casual basis. Generally, except during a formal meeting, we are expected to touch base with colleagues before launching into a discussion about work projects. A simple opening such as "How are you?" or "How's your daughter doing on the volleyball team?" shows a social memory for our workmates and signifies an appreciation for them as whole human beings.

Job-related networking can extend beyond the boundaries of the office. It is not uncommon for coworkers to share a round of golf, go to a basketball game or play a video game together. Through networking, we can also meet people from different companies when there is a crossover between our work friends and our outside friends. This kind of networking can be useful when the time comes to look for a new job. In Silicon Valley and many other places, the best way to seek a job is not by putting out résumés but through networking.

Networking also has the added benefit of building trust among coworkers. Typically, we have a social curiosity about the folks with whom we work. We want to learn a bit more about them and who they are as people, and we want them to show interest in us as well. The more we know about someone, the more we feel we can trust working with that person. It is difficult to collaborate and negotiate with someone we haven't come to trust and know at least a little.

Carol specialized in kids with learning problems. She had a master's degree and was seen as knowledgeable in her field. When she went to advise the teachers about a particular student, she failed to first make a social connection with them. At meetings, she got right to the point and said why her methods should be given preference over strategies that had already been tried. Although she was right and her methods were sound, Carol did not win over the teachers. They found her abrasive, offensive and unfriendly. Carol hadn't figured out the importance and necessity of developing a network to get her thoughts heard. She did not demonstrate any interest in the people she was advising. In turn, they interpreted that she did not respect their previous work with the students. Carol was rejected from the team and put on probation at her job. This pained her greatly.

* * *

Burt took over a managerial role in his company and came in energized with many innovative ideas. He wanted to learn the culture of his company quickly to figure out how to implement change as soon as possible. He met with many higher-ups to discuss his agenda and ask questions about how the business was run. But he soon faced rejection. People described him as odd. They didn't place trust in him, and that made it difficult to get his work done. After more than two years the company let him go, even though he'd been told he accomplished more than anyone in the same position had before. The problem appeared to be his failure to establish social connections. He came in asking questions without first showing any personal interest in the people who would help to answer those questions. Much of language interpretation is by inference; if someone you don't really know comes into your office asking how you've done a certain task in the past, without first making a social connection, you are immediately suspicious about his intentions. Although we all want our companies to succeed, we also want to feel we are part of the process and not being manipulated or used.

* * *

Paul was a very successful lawyer who complained, "Everyone wants to pick my brain about the latest legal update. But no one wants to have lunch with me." Even though Paul was not the one initiating the questions, he still needed to show he was socially interested in the people who sought his advice so that they would want to hang out with him. He would have done well to initiate social chit-chat with others and occasionally ask their opinions on topics as well.

Networking on the job is something that is expected as part of the workday. Of course, it must be done in moderation and should not interfere with work goals. Using technology such as Twitter or Facebook for social networking or purely social reasons is considered recreational and not a good use of company time. An exception might be made for professional networking web sites, such as Linkedin, or similar sites through which members share relevant professional or work-related information.

The goal of networking is to build relationships that help you succeed as part of the work team. That's why taking the time to show an interest in other people's lives is such a central aspect of the workday.

Fitting in and getting along have been important themes in this book. Chapter 8 goes in a slightly different direction by exploring the rules of conduct that are necessary to keep you on the job.

POINTS TO CONSIDER

- ❖ We act in a way that shows we understand what others expect, and that allows them to keep having normal or good thoughts about us.

- ❖ How do we balance who we are—our uniqueness—with the expectations for success at work?

> "Company cultures are like country cultures. Never try to change one. Try, instead, to work with what you've got."
> ~ Peter F. Drucker

> "Be courteous to all, but intimate with few, and let those few be well tried before you give them your confidence."
> ~ George Washington

Chapter 8

Relating at Work
The Office Hierarchy, Friendship, Romance and More

Like any microsociety, work environments have a built-in power structure, that contains an unspoken code and set of hidden rules that apply no matter what the situation. All companies, even the most relaxed, have their own code, and it always includes some kind of hierarchy of personnel to help establish order. The hierarchy is not as much about pecking order as it is about the organization of the company and keeping it running predictably and efficiently.

Often referred to as *office politics*, this aspect of work is one that some people—perhaps new hires or recent college graduates—may not figure out easily. But by learning the code and living according to a company's hidden rules related to personnel, social culture and other areas, you can smooth out the workday and keep your job safe. Each work environment has its own culture; learning this culture is as important as learning the specific tasks you need to do to show proficiency with regards to the job you were hired for.

THE UNSPOKEN CODES AROUND WORKPLACE HIERARCHY AND CULTURE

Asking questions at work is expected, especially at the beginning when you are learning the culture and work expectations. But the frequency of your questions should decrease as you gain experience. Seek advice from managers selectively; the higher up a person's position in the company, the fewer questions he or she is expected to field.

One mistake to avoid is going over the head of the person above you in the hierarchy—for example, your project manager. Not taking your concerns through the proper channels is a quick way to upset the applecart; it may be seen as disrespectful toward the person you report to and a waste of time for the person you approached instead.

Become familiar with the company hierarchy so you know which people in which positions you should go to for certain types of questions. If you're unclear about the chain of command or any other part of the unspoken code or hidden rules, ask the colleague you trust most or your immediate supervisor for direction and advice.

When assigned to a project, you are expected to be as self-reliant as possible and not look for someone to hold your hand. Working independently and reporting occasionally on what you've accomplished are signs of competency, while talking about every detail and seeking constant guidance, reassurance or verbal approval are not.

> Michael was an executive devoted to advancing his career and acquiring knowledge related to his field. Work consumed his life. He made a good impression in the job interview and as a result was hired to work with the company's leaders. As with any high-level job, the company briefed Michael on the current project and encouraged him to develop his own path to meet the project goals. Michael believed he was being diligent by requesting regular

meetings and seeking assurances that he was on the right track. But his superiors perceived him as needy and unproductive, and they let him go after six months.

If you are a salaried professional and are having trouble picking up all the details of your job, it's common and even smart to spend extra time learning during your off-hours. When trying to establish and maintain a career as a salaried professional (unlike a position paid by the hour, where all the learning takes place during work hours), you may need to devote additional time to your work outside the office.

Observing your coworkers can teach you about the company's culture. If people are not bounding out of their chairs to go home at the end of an eight-hour workday, you shouldn't either. However, this does not mean that if other employees are doing something you know is against company custom or policy, such as taking extra-long breaks, that you should follow along.

When taking a break during the day, go ahead and seek out your colleagues for coffee or lunch. If you always work through lunchtime, it may send a message that you don't like your coworkers or are trying to avoid them—even if your intention is to get your work done. You win no friends when you fail to relate to others. And investing time in getting to know your coworkers has payoffs, like having someone who will cover your back when needed, or someone who can just make a dull day more interesting.

Working well with people requires trust, and trust is something you have to build with others. Doing a good job is only one way to show you're someone to be trusted. Asking coworkers for help shows you trust *them*. Another way to create trust is through on-the-job networking, or asking your coworkers about their lives outside of work. You want to stand out as being a hard worker, but also be seen as someone who is making healthy social connections.

THE UNSPOKEN CODES
AROUND FRIENDSHIP, FLIRTING AND ROMANCE

Employers generally encourage work-based friendships, because they help to create employees who are more loyal and connected to the company. It becomes more than simply a place you work—it's a place you want to be because you enjoy the people.

Actively develop friendships at work, but don't let the friendships affect your productivity. Avoid taking extended breaks or making excuses to talk to your friends or hang out at their desks. People notice who is working around the office and who is not. They may even get irritated if it seems like you aren't carrying your weight, and they'll have uncomfortable thoughts and feelings about your persistent off-task behavior. But they probably won't confront you about it—they'll go tell someone else, possibly your supervisor.

Not everyone at work will be a friend, but you should act in a relatively friendly way to everyone. Start by greeting each person when you arrive at work and when you leave each day. Show an interest in your coworkers' lives, and remember what they tell you about themselves—even if you don't consider them friends.

A word on work friendships

Friendships at work can be highly transient. People come and go; things change. You have to put effort into maintaining friendships. Someone doesn't become a friend just because you went on one coffee break together or shared a laugh after a meeting. Work relationships are something you build upon over time.

There are levels of friendship at work, just as there are outside of work. Understanding the different types of relationships in the workplace can help you to interpret your interactions with others, and possibly avoid misunderstandings and misperceptions. Here are some levels of friendship in the workplace:

CLOSE FRIENDS: These are people you spend a lot of time with at work as well as outside of work by mutual agreement. You may confide in them, come to trust them in the workplace and share personal information. You spend time with this person away from the office and engage in conversations and activities that are not work related. It is natural to develop close friends at your job because of how much time you spend there. If one of you leaves your job you will still be considered friends and stay in touch.

OFFICE FRIENDS: These are people you are very friendly with at work. You may spend your break times with them and have lunch together, but typically you don't communicate outside of work on a regular basis unrelated to work questions. You may see them once in a while at a work party, or during a get-together with other office friends, but usually you don't confide in office friends. It is expected that you will make a number of office friends over the course of your time with a company. If you leave the company it is unlikely you will stay in close touch with office friends, but you can use them for networking now and in the future.

OFFICE ACQUAINTANCES: You are friendly to many people at work. You know their names and a little bit about their lives, but you don't spend much time with them during the workday. You don't go out of your way to seek out office acquaintances, but when you happen upon them in the hall or lunchroom, you are friendly and you may engage them in small talk. You talk to them mostly in passing, and you also occasionally engage in small talk. Sometimes you simply greet them; other times you might ask how they are, how their weekend went, whether they have plans for the evening, and so on. Office acquaintances are also people who may put in a good word for you as they are loosely part of your network.

SOMEWHAT FRIENDLY BUT NOT FRIENDS: These are people you see in your work area and acknowledge with a greeting, but beyond that you don't really know who they are. Over time you may learn their names and roles in the company, but typically you don't talk to them. If you were to show an interest in one of these persons and engage in some level of small talk with them, they would then become office acquaintances. People you greet, and are somewhat friendly to, are not usually helpful when it comes to networking; they simply don't know you well enough.

For those who have never had a real chance to make friends, the work environment may provide the first opportunity to work closely with a group of people over time. But the lack of earlier experience in forming close friendships or interpreting people's thoughts and intentions may stymie any efforts to develop relationships on the job. In Chapter 11 we will review some strategies to consider to help you progress from being somewhat friendly into an acquaintance, etc.

> Henry had worked part time for an accounting agency for over twenty years. For most of those years he came in, did his tasks and went home. He didn't talk to people and had no friends; he would not even be considered somewhat friendly. When he became aware of his loneliness, he sought our help. We taught him how to appear friendlier at work and how to start forming acquaintances. Henry applied these strategies to show he was interested in his coworkers. As a result, Mary became an office acquaintance. She and Henry greeted each other during the day, and he began small-talk conversations at her cubicle about her life outside of work. She was reliably friendly, although they did not go out to lunch together or share coffee breaks.
>
> Each winter for many years Henry had gone to Hawaii by himself. He thought it would be more fun to travel with a companion, so he approached Mary and asked if she'd like to accompany him that winter. Mary politely turned him down, but she was very uncomfortable with the invitation. Henry did not realize that asking a single woman to travel to a distant city implied that he wanted to take their

relationship to an intimate level and presumably share a hotel room and a bed.

Henry insisted to us that his invitation was strictly about wanting company when in Hawaii. We explained that his reality was not necessarily Mary's perception, and that it was necessary to go through the stages of friendship to build trust. Only then would Mary know Henry well enough to be able to discuss the trip, or at least to get reliable cues about Henry's true intentions.

A word on flirting and romance [2]

Romantic interests in the workplace are tricky to navigate. If you do become romantically involved with someone at work, you should be aware that there's an additional code of behavior—one that you are responsible for knowing, as many companies have written rules for appropriate social conduct. These rules explicitly state the behaviors that constitute the legal definition of sexual harassment, which is discussed in the next section.

It's not uncommon for people who work together to develop deeper and sometimes romantic interests in each other. After all, work is where we spend most of our time. But be aware that flirting and romance can distract you from your tasks and affect your productivity. If a relationship does develop between two employees at work, and they begin dating it must be understood that any kind of display of affection or intimacy at work makes other employees uncomfortable and generally is not allowed. And, if they break up or have a fight, this can take a toll on both of them and may cause work problems. Often the issue of greatest concern to employers is that employees who are romantically involved may lose their professional objectivity and be unable to judge each other's work fairly. Things can get complicated pretty quickly.

---

2   The information that follows in this chapter, like all information in this book, is not intended as legal guidance, instead it is general information. We strongly recommend readers learn, from the company that employs them, their company's stated policy as related to sexual harassment.

The company has a stake in the relationship, too—it has invested time and money to hire and train employees. If a relationship is in trouble, it can cause emotions to run high at work or even cause someone to quit. These challenges have a direct impact on the company and your coworkers as well.

THE UNSPOKEN CODES AROUND SEXUAL BEHAVIOR AND BULLYING

A word on sexual harassment

Sometimes you develop a crush on a coworker but the feeling is *not* reciprocal. You must always read the cues to make sure you recognize when this is the situation and *tread carefully*; you don't want to violate any sexual harassment laws. Sexual harassment is a form of sex discrimination that happens in the workplace. The U.S. Equal Employment Opportunity Commission defines it as unwelcome or uninvited sexual conduct that is severe or pervasive and affects working conditions or creates a hostile or offensive work environment.

What you might think of as flirting with a coworker can be considered sexual harassment. Avoid all jokes about, comments on and references to a person's body, gender or sexuality in the workplace. Occasionally you can compliment someone with a general comment such as "You look nice today" or "I like that color on you." But if you tell a coworker she looks sexy in her outfit or you get too personal by saying, "You look hot today—are you going on a date with someone?" these comments will probably make him or her feel uneasy and even sexually harassed. You must be even more careful if you are in a position of authority because one determinant of sexual harassment is if the employee feels intimidated in the work environment or feels his or her job is being compromised.

Don't think sexual harassment is just words. Showing someone images or graphics of a sexual nature can be harassing, and you can also harass people by how you act. You can even be accused of sexual harassment for looking too long or staring at someone's body, or spending too much time looking like you're *thinking* about the other person.

Few people would acknowledge themselves to be a stalker. But certain behaviors can easily be misinterpreted as stalking. Although a strict interpretation is "unwanted actions or conduct that put a person in fear for his or her safety," a more commonplace understanding of stalking is giving someone a lot of attention when the attention is not reciprocated. The person may feel she is being stalked if you watch her, see when she is taking a break and follow her, attempt to talk to her throughout the day, get her phone number, text, send personal e-mails or call him or her at home without permission. These are not the behaviors of someone who is just trying to be friendly. *You have to notice whether the other person welcomes the attention.* If she fails to talk to you, actively appears to avoid you or pay attention to you, tells you she does not want to talk by phone, doesn't answer repeated e-mails, or always has an excuse for not going out with you after work, *back off*. Even if *you* believe your intentions are friendly, if she interprets them as stalking or sexual harassment, you could be getting yourself into hot water and a sexual harassment complaint or lawsuit could be headed your way.

Many companies offer training to increase awareness and prevent sexual harassment. It would be prudent to research the topic online to learn more about it. It's the kind of information you're responsible for knowing and following; saying you didn't realize you were harassing someone is not an acceptable excuse.

The definition of *sexual behavior* is based on perception, interpretation and inference. Awareness of how others might perceive your actions and words is critical; this is what social thinking is all about!

Keeping in mind the hazards of sexual harassment in the workplace, if there's someone you think you might like, treat that person the way you would any coworker you want to know better, by showing a personal interest. (For ideas on conversation topics, see Chapter 7.) If a close friendship develops and then continues outside the office (by mutual agreement), that is where any sexual behavior—intimacy, touching, very personal comments— needs to take place.

Even if someone agrees to go out with you outside of work (or during a lunch break), and you think that means she is sexually interested in you, still be careful in interpreting his or her intentions, and be prepared to back off immediately!

- **Listen to the words.** The code language for not wanting to advance to a sexual relationship is something like, "I really think you are nice, but I just want to be your friend."
- **Read the cues.** Nonverbal cues that the person does not want to be more intimate include—not reaching out to hold your hand as you put it across the table, looking around the room while you stare at him or her, not bending in toward you and even moving away, and not looking you directly in the eye. (One of the first ways we flirt with our bodies is with lingering, direct eye contact.)

A word on bullying in the workplace

While it would be nice to think the days of cliques and bullies ended in middle and high school, the reality is that these social structures and tactics of exclusion exist in the workplace, although they are more subtle.

Work is a reliable place to meet people and make friends. Social groups at work (and elsewhere) provide a sense of belonging. But sometimes groups form that seem like schoolyard cliques. Gossip is one way people relate to each other, and it makes them feel as if they are part of an inner circle or in the know. The bonds in social groups can become so strong that newcomers don't feel welcome. At its worst, social exclusion can become a source of conflict and division in the workplace.

Just as in school, where there were kids who didn't know how to make friends, there will be people in your office who do not develop friendships easily, even though they want to connect. Maybe they exhibit a less desirable social trait (for example, they talk too much or don't get to the point) that makes others uncomfortable. Just as in school, people tend to make fun of those who seem different from them. And just as in school, people rarely tell someone what they think about him but do go tell ten of their friends. This results in a bunch of people talking about one person that no one is talking to.

While this book is dedicated to providing information about social expectations and social thinking in the workplace, it is also is meant to acknowledge the many talented folks in the working world who weren't born already wired with the ability to learn social thinking and related social skills. They feel the frustration of not being included, and in fact have felt it their whole lives. Many of them keep trying the strategies that will allow them greater social success, but the nuances of communication and the nonverbal world are complex and confusing. These individuals are not purposely trying to create uncomfortable thoughts in others; they just do.

These folks, who are considered a bit odd, are often excluded and prevented from entering social groups at work. People bully them in subtle ways—for instance, monitoring them closely and reporting everything they do wrong to management, excluding them from parties or ganging up as a show of force to try and get them fired.

> Rudy was an office manager responsible for purchasing decisions for the company's reference library. Martha, an employee, disagreed with one of his decisions but was overruled. About a year later, Rudy told another employee that she needed to be more productive. This employee happened to be one of Martha's close friends, and together with some other coworkers in their social group they filed a complaint with management, claiming that Rudy had used poor judgment in his decision-making for the library. Rudy was called in to explain himself. Although Rudy was aware of the hardball tactics Martha and her friends were using and knew it was about a year-old grudge, he was not able to convince the management that these employees were trying to get even. Instead he ended up

having to defend his purchase decisions at length, even though the real issue was a power struggle between Rudy and the clique of employees he supervised. The managers did not see what he saw, nor had they shared his experience. Martha and her circle were perceived as friendly workers, while Rudy had made far fewer social connections. That gave Martha a stronger voice with the managers and put Rudy on the defensive, although his professional judgment had been sound all along.

Although we consider bullying a negative aspect of the school playground, adults in the workforce dole out their fair share of collective bullying when they feel a coworker has not been sensitive to the group mindset, and certain employees will use tactics to exclude those who don't follow the social norms. And just as we would report bullies in the schoolyard, we need to stand up for people at work who may not have as much social savvy. We are all responsible for each other. When we become aware of abusive or unfair treatment, we need to report it to a person in management when coworkers are setting others up for failure or simply making fun of someone they work with because they have a lower social status. Here's a suggestion—Go out of your way to befriend a person who may not be the social butterfly at work. You will often find a caring, creative person who lacks natural social sophistication but is an incredibly interesting and thoughtful person nevertheless.

As people who have dedicated our careers to those with social learning challenges, it is painful for us to hear their stories of rejection and loneliness. As one of my clients told me, "The loneliest place in the world is being by yourself in a room where everyone is friendly with each other, just not with you."

In the next chapter, we will look at the intricacies of electronic communication and technology in the workplace, and how they are revolutionizing the way—but not the reasons why—we socialize and connect with each other, on both a personal and professional level.

Good Intentions Are Not Good Enough

POINTS TO CONSIDER

❖ Someone doesn't become a friend just because you went on one coffee break together or shared a laugh after a meeting. Work relationships are something you build upon over time.

❖ What you might think of as flirting with a co-worker can be considered sexual harassment.

www.dilbert.com, ©1991 United Feature Syndicate, Inc.

> "Electric communication will never be a substitute for the face of someone who with their soul encourages another person to be brave and true."
> ~ Charles Dickens

> "The newest computer can merely compound, at speed, the oldest problem in the relations between human beings, and in the end the communicator will be confronted with the old problem, of what to say and how to say it."
> ~ Edward R. Murrow

Chapter 9

Social Technology
How It's Changing
the Way We Communicate

Technology is ever-present and ever-changing, offering faster and more interesting ways to entertain, teach, inform, captivate and distract us. Few of us have time to keep up with the increasing demands of technology or to manage the overwhelming number of available options. But we keep on trying!

In the workplace, technology has its upside and downside. Although it provides tools to make work more efficient, it also provides a handy way to avoid it. Employees can surf the Internet, keep an eye on the news, answer personal e-mail, plan a vacation or read favorite blogs, all while giving the appearances of doing actual work.

More importantly, technology has changed how people communicate. The Internet spurred a communication revolution, adding a whole new layer of social behavior to human culture. E-mail, texting, instant messaging (IM), social networking and online chats are ways we now can connect with others. Because these technologies are still relatively young modes of communication, rules for expected behavior are still evolving—whether we are online making personal connections, maintaining professional contacts or taking brain breaks at our desks.

A word on staying focused

Many companies, well aware of the *brain drain* the Internet can be in the workplace, have written usage policies. In a recent survey, 54 percent of companies reported that they prohibit employees from using social-media sites while on the job. Some employers use technology to monitor workers' productivity and how they're spending their time online. But whether a policy is in writing or not, in the end the best person to supervise your Internet usage is *you*. As in eating junk food, it only becomes a problem if you don't monitor your consumption.

The key is self-discipline. While it is reasonable to take short breaks at your desk, it may be difficult to log off quickly once you've gotten onto an interesting web site. Avoid tempting yourself, and don't start something you can't stop easily.

It is important to note that certain types of sites need to be avoided at all times, even if you are on your break time. For example, sites with sexually explicit information are *never* acceptable on a work-owned computer, even if you are using it outside the office.

It is critical that you become familiar with the Internet and e-mail policies where you work. Some companies explicitly state allowed uses during the workday. If you aren't sure what the policies are, don't make assumptions; ask if there are any restrictions on or rules for computer use. And always keep in mind that the company owns the computers and the network, and you must use them in ways the company intends. If you don't, and you violate policy, it can be grounds for discipline or firing.

A word on Internet distractions

Many adults have very active social lives via the Internet. For some with social learning challenges who find face to face interactions the most challenging of all, they invest great time and energy connecting with others via the web. In fact, virtual friendships, chats, instant messaging, social networking sites and other forms of online communication may represent the majority of some people's daily social interactions, other than strictly job-related conversations during the day. The Internet also gives access to more solitary enjoyments, such as playing games, reading blogs and news or watching video clips.

The truth is, few of us can say we have never used work-based access to the Internet for our own personal, social or recreational interests. So how do we stay on task, follow the expected behaviors and social rules of computer use, and resist the temptation to get preoccupied or "lost" online?

Some people have alerts sent to their computers from news or entertainment sites. Even if you don't take specific, designated breaks to cruise the Internet, you still may be getting too distracted if you find yourself frequently interrupted by pop-up announcements, e-mails and the like. Remember that you are being paid to be productive throughout the workday.

Of course, everyone has downtimes, but don't be lured into spending yours online. Most employers prefer that workers use their break time socializing in the office and not playing on the computer. They know that work-based friendships help to promote teamwork and lead to a stronger commitment to the job.

It's not just the company that cares about how you use your computer. People who work together all pay attention to what those around them are doing, and they notice who is less productive. If you don't appear to be carrying your share of the workload, you will come under more scrutiny. Anytime coworkers walk by and see you sitting in front of your computer, they'll assume you're working—and you should be!

A word on e-mail and saying what's on your mind

If you work in an office, communicating by e-mail, text or some other form of IM is prevalent, sometimes even if the intended recipient is sitting right next to you.

There are many advantages to posting your questions or comments, project outlines and updates in an electronic format. It is a highly efficient form of communication. It provides a way to track a project and review or clarify details along the way. And, if something ever goes wrong, a chain of e-mails can also be pulled up to determine the cause.

The good news is that e-mail and IM are fast, concrete, visual and readily available. That is also the bad news. People can easily get in trouble for using these technologies inappropriately. One employee in our office was found to be sending job applications, e-mailing potential new employers and doing phone interviews—all on company time and using company property. It did *not* go over well with the management! In a more prominent example, a congressman from Florida was forced to resign in 2006 after he was caught sending sexually explicit IMs to teenage boys.

When sending professional e-mails, be careful not to complain about fellow coworkers or work-related concerns. All too often, the message can get buried within another e-mail and sent to someone else, who finds your original message simply by reading through the history. Your negative comments can then be forwarded to others, and next thing you know you're having to explain yourself. E-mails are often forwarded and taken out of context.

The rules for business-related e-mail also apply to online chatting and IMing. Be aware that these are documented conversations that can be sent on to others.

If you are having a conflict with a person at work, expressing your upset feelings in an e-mail is not the best way to work this out. Given the speed of electronic communication, we may act more impulsively when responding to people via e-mail than we would if we were face-to-face. It's a mistake to think that e-mail simplifies angry or heated exchanges; in fact, it often exacerbates them. If you're upset with someone, a good old-fashioned discussion is still the best way to handle it.

We all get irritated and sometimes even angry with people at work. When you vent in person to close friends, it is most often off the record and stays private. As soon as you post your feelings in e-mail, on a blog or web site, you put them on the record, where they easily can be passed along to others. Blogs and social media sites are not necessarily private, and in some cases they are very public. Even on a social networking site like Facebook that has privacy settings, you must be discreet about what you express. If you put your thoughts in writing, anyone can share them with others.

If you are communicating anger, it doesn't matter if you believe your feelings are justified because you felt someone "did you wrong." If your behavior and temperament make others uncomfortable, you may be seen as a difficult employee. Remember how in school, if someone punched the bully back he would get in as much if not more trouble than the bully himself?

The bottom line: Even if you write on your own time, away from the office, on your own computer, you are responsible—they are still *your* thoughts. You own the thoughts, and you are choosing to share them with others, but you can never fully choose how people will interpret them once they are posted.

A word on expected behavior (it still applies!)

For individuals with social learning challenges, electronic media offer easier ways to interact because they require interpreting only written language and not the facial expression, tone of voice and gestures that are part of more complex face-to-face interactions. If you lag in processing and responding to spoken language, online communication also allows for those valuable extra few seconds to help get your thoughts together and form a more organized, coherent response.

Online communication definitely has advantages and can be an excellent way to communicate—as long as you use it as *expected,* not only with your coworkers but in all your personal and professional communication.

Here are a few common sense ideas for using the Internet, texting and game-playing:

1. Avoid tempting yourself by keeping a web page open on your browser behind your active work. You will get distracted, and coworkers may notice that you quickly shift your screen back to "work mode" as they walk by.
2. Texting is another form of technology, although not computer-based, that can pull you away from work. Set

a limit on the number of times a day you text with your kids, friends or spouse. If you find yourself frequently responding to or initiating text messages, think about setting boundaries, because even though each text may be quick, you are most likely getting sidetracked.

3. Avoid blogging about anything related to work—not only about people you work with, but projects you work on and your company in general. Any information created during working hours or related directly to your job is owned by the company and is not to be shared without permission. Any comments stated after work hours that paint your company or employees of your company in a negative light can cause you significant problems.

   Be careful what you post on social networking sites. They are not as private as you think. Although in many states employers are not supposed to look on public sites, they do. A twenty-five-year-old employee taught his older coworkers how to use MySpace (the social networking site) to screen applicants for entry-level jobs; he was able to quickly access a remarkable amount of negative information (for example, illicit drug use, frequent drinking binges) that resulted in the business discontinuing its interest in a number of otherwise promising applicants.

4. Stay away from computer gaming sites, role-playing games, Second Life, online chats or anything unrelated to work that grabs your attention during the day. It's easy to lose control of your time and get engrossed by a compelling web site.

Despite living in the age of technology, human communication hasn't changed all that much. We still yearn for connection and need to be thoughtful about what we say and how we say it, consider the situation and the people in it, try to interpret meaning and follow social rules that ultimately determine how we get along with others. The ways we communicate today may be different, but the reasons are pretty much the same!

POINTS TO CONSIDER

❖ Anytime coworkers walk by and see you sitting in front of your computer, they'll assume you're working—and you should be!

❖ Avoid tempting yourself with non work related distractions and don't start something you can't stop easily.

> "There's only one corner of the universe you can be certain
> of improving, and that's your own self."
> ~ Aldous Huxley

Chapter 10

Social Behavior Maps (SBM) for Adults Navigating the Social-Emotional Terrain

In Chapter One we learned that one definition of *good social skills* is related to understanding the social expectations of a situation—the hidden rules—and not about following a behavioral formula all the time.

For instance, when walking through the night markets of Hong Kong, the only way to avoid constant harassment by the street vendors is to turn your face away from them and intentionally walk away while they're talking to you. In this situation, walking away is the expected norm and the socially accepted way of showing disinterest. Berating each street vendor who tries to sell you his products would be perceived as rude. Although both behaviors would have the same outcome, only one is considered socially appropriate.

As this example demonstrates, good social skills aren't necessarily about acting nice or upbeat at all times; they are more about doing what is expected, which helps to keep people in our presence calm.

Every encounter has a social-emotional component. In fact, simply being around other people, even without direct interaction, can alter each person's mood and behavioral responses.

A treatment framework Winner developed called Social Behavior Mapping helps to explore the complicated act of social interpretation in an objective, unemotional way. It provides an explanation for how different behaviors (expected and unexpected) result in an evaluation of one's intentions, which then leads to emotional responses and related behavioral responses. It is a visual method for observing and analyzing the cause-and-effect of social interactions, detailing concretely how each person's behavior sets off a chain of emotions (usually predictable) and behavioral responses (good and bad).

Simply put, the Social Behavior Map looks at how our behavior affects people, how these people then interpret the behavior, how they respond to their feelings about the behavior and how their responses affect us.

The Social Behavior Map ties together some of the concepts of social communication, such as the Social-Emotional Chain Effect. You will recognize several core principles of social thinking in the following steps, which break down the process of communication and show how all the pieces connect. (See the template and samples from pages 162–167 to organize your thinking around these ideas.)

SITUATION OR CONTEXT: Describe briefly at the top of the map the specific situation you are exploring—in other words, the basis for why people are reacting and responding to you in the way they are.

EXPECTED OR/UNEXPECTED BEHAVIORS YOU PRODUCE: List behaviors in the expected or unexpected columns based on the hidden rules for the situation being explored.

HOW THE OBSERVER INTERPRETS THE INTENTIONS OF THE BEHAVIOR: Each social behavior is interpreted to have meaning, hence the reason we call it a "social behavior." Define how others interpreted the intentions of the person producing the expected or unexpected behavior.

FEELINGS OF OTHERS: Name the basic emotions people might feel about your expected or unexpected behaviors.

CONSEQUENCES: Describe the reactions or behavioral responses people produced based on the emotional response to your behaviors, positive or negative.

YOUR FEELINGS: Note your own emotional response based on how people treated you behaviorally, based on how they felt about your initial behaviors, expected and unexpected.

The Social Behavior Map is a relatively simple system for thinking about the overly abstract topic of how we relate and respond to each other.

Many of us feel awkward talking about social behavior and how it connects to our emotions. The Social Behavior Map allows for the discussion to evolve in a more direct, matter-of-fact way. The SBM for adults is different from the version provided to school age students in that it adds a column to explore how people interpret behaviors through exploring the implied or interpreted intentions. The maps provide a visual review that can help cement the importance of social relationships in and outside the workplace. By providing a succinct way to explore the social challenges encountered in any work environment, the maps help us to focus on the core information.

The insights gleaned through the maps can be difficult to put into words, because the information in them is usually processed intuitively. It is helpful to think of each map as a magnifying glass used to more closely observe the intense, highly emotional framework of the work environment.

There is a growing awareness of the importance of emotions at work ("Managing Emotions in the Workplace," Knowledge@Wharton, April 2007; http://tinyurl.com/workplace-emotions).

In the workplace, active displays of unfriendliness or anger are unexpected. As adults we are supposed to be able to identify and deal with our emotions calmly. Although negative emotions have their rightful place in our lives, they are mostly felt and not expressed publicly. In order for people to feel they can work well together, the majority of interactions are expected to produce emotional responses ranging from neutral to positive (this is called *emotional expression compression*).

A young adult who created an SBM to analyze a difficult social situation described the *expected behavior* side of the map as "a tornado of daisies." He said, "When I do what's expected, people feel good, they treat me well, I feel better about myself and I then treat people even better." In contrast, he referred to the *unexpected behavior* side of the map as "a tornado of *%*#," and observed that when he does the unexpected, people get upset, they treat him badly, that makes him mad and then he treats people even worse.

Social Behavior Mapping demonstrates that any time our social behavior is interpreted as having positive intentions, this makes others around us feel good, and inevitably they will treat us better. This positive feedback is one of the things that drives altruistic behavior—the practice of acting in an unselfish way purely to benefit others. At the same time, the SBM demonstrates that truly altruistic behavior is rare, given that any time we act with kindness or behave in ways that make others feel good, they treat us better in return.

We encourage you to map out some of the social contexts you find to be challenging and to visually dissect each one. What appears to be an overwhelming and complex situation may not seem so hard to handle when you break it down this way.

FOLLOW THESE STEPS TO DEVELOP AND USE A SOCIAL BEHAVIOR MAP

1. Identify the problematic situation.

2. Begin by naming the unexpected behaviors first (we're so much better at figuring out what people do wrong rather than noticing what they do right!). Keep the list to five or fewer behaviors. If you are unsure which behaviors are unexpected, ask for assistance from a trusted friend or supervisor.

3. Using words rather than sentences, describe how the observer interpreted the intentions of the unexpected behavior.

4. List related emotions (again by using words rather than sentences) that these interpreted intentions triggered.

5. Cite specific ways in which the observer reacts after having had a negative emotional response. Describe the office procedures that now need to be put into place based on the negative emotions elicited. These are the natural consequences.

6. Describe how this information makes the person who produced the unexpected behavior feel about himself—if his is willing to talk about it in that moment. (If he is not willing to talk about it, let it go.)

7. Now move to the expected side of the map. Take the originally described unexpected behaviors, and now list the expected version of each of these unexpected behaviors. For example, if an unexpected behavior is "Does not acknowledge others' ideas in meetings," the expected behavior would be "Positively acknowledges others' ideas."

8. Describe in words rather than sentences describe how the observer interpreted the intentions of the unexpected behavior.

9. List related emotions (again by using words rather than sentences) that these interpreted intentions triggered. (On this side of the map, the triggered emotions are usually positive.)

10. Based on the emotional response, give examples of related behavioral responses (positive consequences), which can be as simple as a calm face, calm voice, small smile.

11. Describe how this information emotionally impacts the person who produced the expected behaviors.

12. Once the map is completed, illuminate points by drawing a circle around key words in each column and then using lines to connect the circles, demonstrating the cause-and-effect relationship of everyone on the map. See pages 166-167.

13. Privately review the maps before reengaging in the negative contexts or/situations that a person finds challenging.

Good Intentions Are Not Good Enough

Use the following templates and sample Social Behavior Maps to work through the process to help you understand social-emotional behavior and responses. If you find it difficult to create your own maps, you can use the samples that have specific situations most of us encounter during the workday. You can also use the samples to think through similar situations you encounter throughout your day.

No one is perfect at social interpretation—everyone makes mistakes.

Social Behavior Mapping for Adults

Situation: _____

What is Expected for this situation

Your Expected Behavior	Perceived Intentions: How others interpret the intentions of your behavior	How the interpreted intentions make other people feel	How others react to their related feelings (consequences)	How the reactions make you feel

Good Intentions Are Not Good Enough

What is Unexpected for this situation

Your Unexpected Behavior	Perceived Intentions: How others interpret the intentions of your behavior	How the interpreted intentions make other people feel	How others react to their related feelings (consequences)	How the reactions make you feel

Social Behavior Mapping for Adults

Situation: *Collaborating with Colleagues at Work*

What is Expected for this situation

Your Expected Behavior	Perceived Intentions: How others interpret the intentions of your behavior	How the interpreted intentions make other people feel	How others react to their related feelings. (consequences)	How the reactions make you feel
Asking colleagues for help Seek assistance from individual peers when brainstorming an idea or when stuck or confused at work. Seek advice from supervisors who are knowledgeable about what you are developing. At meetings, encourage people to elaborate on your ideas by giving their input. Acknowledge to your peers (individually and even in a meeting) that you don't have all the answers and enjoy working with them.	Respect for others ideas and experiences. Demonstrating respect for Supervisor's knowledge. Respect for the people in the meeting. Demonstrating you appreciate that others have different knowledge sets or experiences than you do.	Respected Good Included Appreciated Intelligent	Include you in their problem-solving, which leads to team building. Seek you out to further share and discuss ideas. Extend networking opportunities because they see you as a person who respects their ideas. Demonstrate respect for your knowledge. See you as someone who collaborates and works as a team.	Happy Proud Included

Good Intentions Are Not Good Enough

Social Behavior Mapping for Adults

Situation: *Collaborating with Colleagues at Work*

What is Unexpected for this situation

Your Unexpected Behavior	Perceived Intentions: How others interpret the intentions of your behavior	How the interpreted intentions make other people feel	How others react to their related feelings. (consequences)	How the reactions make you feel
Not asking colleagues for help.	Don't appreciate others' knowledge or experiences.	Rejected	Ignore you. Act unfriendly (with words, facial expression, tone of voice).	Mad
Do all idea development in isolation, not consulting others who may have relevant knowledge.	You want to prove you are better than they are.	Irritated	Avoid asking you to be on the team or work in groups.	Hurt
Tell people only what you know, never letting on what you don't know.	Avoid wanting to be a member of a team.	Insulted	Tell others they find you annoying.	Frustrated
Don't tell supervisors when you run into problems, and instead convince yourself you have it under control.	Don't like people you work with.	Stressed	Refuse to give you full credit for your ideas because you did not work as a team.	Stressed
Discourage people from contributing to your idea/proposal.				Rejected

Social Behavior Mapping for Adults

Situation: *Sharing your thoughts/ideas in a meeting*

What is Expected for this situation

Your Expected Behavior	Perceived Intentions: How others interpret the intentions of your behavior	How the interpreted intentions make other people feel	How others react to their related feelings. (consequences)	How the reactions make you feel
Connect your ideas to ones that were previously presented.	Relating ideas, showing approval of others' ideas.	Calm	Give you more positive/supportive responses when you are sharing ideas.	Respected
Crystallize your explanation to focus on the most efficient way to communicate your point.	Respectful of others' knowledge of time constraints.	Respected	More likely to consider your input during other times.	Good
Support others' ideas even if you think privately that their ideas are not as good as yours.	Relationship building.	Pleased	See you as a positive member of the team.	Included
Be attentive (with your eyes and body) by using signals of active listening: Look toward the speaker and keep your body/trunk subtly turned toward the speaker.	Respect for person who is speaking. Attentive, Interested.		Seek your opinion and want to run ideas by you during less formal work discussions, or invite you out socially (luchtime, after work get togethers.)	Appreciated Calm

Good Intentions Are Not Good Enough

Social Behavior Mapping for Adults

Situation: *Sharing your thoughts/ideas in a meeting*

What is Unexpected for this situation

Your Unexpected Behavior	Perceived Intentions: How others interpret the intentions of your behavior	How the interpreted intentions make other people feel	How others react to their related feelings. (consequences)	How the reactions make you feel
Say what you're thinking without much, if any, connection to the current topic.	You're not listening to what others are saying.	Frustrated	Tell you your ideas are not related or relevant to the current discussion and discount what you're saying, even if your ideas have value.	Disrespected
Provide too much detail oriented background information to build up to your main idea, without considering the group's prior knowledge about the topic or need to know this level of detail.	You're demonstrating that you know more than the others.	Irritated		Frustrated
	You do not appreciate the time based demands of others.	Disrespected	Unable to follow your train of thought, they interrupt and urge you to get to the point, or later tell you privately that you have to work on being more succinct at meetings.	Mad
				Disengaged
Ignore others' ideas, or worse, suggest their ideas are not good enough and that they should listen to yours.	The person who does this thinks they are superior to me (us)!	Exasperated	Dismiss what you say, since you dismiss what they say.	Isolated
Appear lost in thought when others are talking.	You're not interested in others, only interested in your own thinking.		Fail to see you as a team player.	

POINTS TO CONSIDER

❖ Others interpret your intentions based on their own thinking. You cannot decide how your intentions are interpreted. If you think you have good intentions, this does not mean people would agree with you.

❖ Any time your social behavior is interpreted as leading to good intentions, inevitably people will treat you better. Even if you made a mistake, if they interpret your intentions as good, they will be kinder and guide you through the problem solving process rather than blaming you!

❖ Remember, no one is perfect at social interpretation—everyone makes mistakes.

❖ While the visual charting of Social Behavior Mapping helps define and systematize the cause and effect of social emotional reactions and responses, as you consider this information you may find it helpful to simply talk with others in this more systematic way. When discussing or considering your own behaviors (expected or/unexpected), ask people how they interpreted your intentions, how this made them feel, and then discuss whether this is why you observed them treating you in a specific way. The more people encourage an explicit conversation about social emotional communication, the more clearly people can discuss this information. If you simply say to other persons, "Why don't you like me?" or "Why did you treat me so badly?" they will be less likely to be able to explain the source of their own behavioral reaction.

Chapter 11

Strategies: Tips and Pointers

Learning social thinking and related social skills does not begin with getting us to just go change our behavior, although that is often the message well-meaning clinicians, parents and employers convey. A better method is for us to become more acute observers of the social world and its many entwined expectations. In a moment of social interaction, so many things are happening at once—body language, facial expression, physical presence, language, tone and volume of voice. In order to explore this process we actually have to break it apart to be able to learn to see the trees within the forest.

Many of the tips and pointers reviewed in this chapter are to develop the increased self-awareness needed for us to begin to slowly alter our related behaviors; this is referred to in the world of treatment as *cognitive behavior therapy*. Stephen Briers' book titled *Brilliant Cognitive Behavioural Therapy: How to Use CBT to Improve Your Mind and Your Life* does a good job explaining the basic tenets of this treatment approach in a very user-friendly format. Cognitive behavioral therapy is a process in which you modify how you think about a specific set of information to modify how you react behaviorally to that information. Most of us can understand that if you want to change your eating habits, you don't just go and do it because you say you want to do it. Instead, you begin to rethink what you are eating and if it is nutritious and good for your health. As you learn about what you want to put in your body, you change your food intake behaviors by thinking about what you have learned about food.

To help change your social behaviors, as pointed out in the previous chapters in this book, you have to begin by rethinking how you approach and then respond to the many and varied aspects that create what we refer to as social communication. It is helpful to acknowledge your problems to a trusted friend who you can repeatedly check in with.

TIPS AND POINTERS BASED ON INFORMATION IN CHAPTER 1

- **Social Thinking Versus Social Skills. Thinking about thinking socially.**

    Begin the process by simply observing your own mind. Recognize that you think about what you are expected to do before you do it, given that you want people to understand what you are trying to convey. The *thinking* part of this process is what we call *social thinking*; the behaviors you use to convey your message are what people refer to as *social skills*. Simply try to observe your own brain at work. Even if you are known to have problems with producing appropriate social skills, you still are doing this process to some extent.

    Over time the goal is to learn how to adjust your thinking to help you adjust your social skills; however, this process takes time. Realize you have practiced one way to think about the experience of the social mind for as many years as you have been alive. If you are forty-five years old, you have practiced this thinking for nearly forty-five years; therefore, you are not going to adapt quickly to these ideas. Allow yourself time, and you may choose to have others read this so they are also a bit more patient with your learning process.

- **Social Emotional Memory**

    Explore your own social emotional memory system. Observe how it works. Think about whether you truly remember exactly what people have said to you, or if you capture more memories related to how people feel. Many adults I have worked with have challenges in learning how to perceive and respond to others' emotions, yet they are highly emotionally responsive people themselves. Valuing how their own emotional systems work can help to validate how others emotions work as well. As mentioned in this book, how one person reacts and responds to information is likely how another will react and respond, even with people who have social learning challenges.

TIPS AND POINTERS BASED ON INFORMATION IN CHAPTER 2

- **Strategies for social communication. Observe social psychology in action in your own brain.**

    Review this basic chain effect related to our social psychology as presented below. It is very likely that you will notice these tenets hold true in your own brain. If so, this will be a thought process you will want to review and consider, as it is at the heart of why we work so hard to monitor what people are possibly thinking, and we adapt our own social skills to meet their needs. After all, if this is how we think, then it makes sense others have these same internal feelings.

    ❖ We all want others to have reasonable or good thoughts about us as often as possible.

    ❖ We all worry that others don't like us.

    ❖ We all have to focus on trying to make those around us feel OK, even when we don't plan to interact.

    ❖ We all have to be aware that people try to read our intentions, but we cannot be sure they are reading them accurately. We need to monitor how others are thinking in order to ensure that we are having reasonable reciprocal social thoughts about each other.

- ❖ We all have to monitor and possibly adjust our behavior to make it more likely people are reading our intentions the way we want them to be read. For example, we may have to look attentive when we're feeling bored, act as if we are interested in someone's idea so he or she will consider our idea or simply say "Hi" in a friendly tone of voice even when someone is irritating us!

- **Analyze what are the expected and unexpected behaviors in any given situation**

    Document a specific situation in which you are in the presence of other people.

    - ❖ On paper make two columns; on one side write "expected behaviors," and on the other side write "unexpected behaviors."

    - ❖ Observe the situation.

    - ❖ Write down your observations of people doing what is unexpected in this situation and some behaviors you imagine that would be unexpected. Ask your advisor what other unexpected behaviors might occur. A *behavior* is any type of behavior produced by the body including language, facial expression or physical presence.

    - ❖ Write down your observations of some expected behaviors as well, especially as they relate to the unexpected behaviors. For example, based on what you list as "unexpected," now consider what would be the expected version of that behavior as described in this chapter.

For more on this topic read the book called, *The Hidden Curriculum* by Brenda Smith Myles, Melissa L. Trautman, and Ronda L. Schelvan (2004; Autism Asperger Publishing: Kansas.)

- **Explore how social nuance is expressed in the following areas:**

    Stated Time Demands: Observe how others talk about their time demands, and explore how you respond or if you respond to others' subtle acknowledgements that they have limited time to talk. Work on increasing your sensitivity for listening to these types of comments if you have not been aware of their importance previously. *Increasing sensitivity* means that you adjust your behavior by shortening your verbal response without acting in an irritated manner when people allude to their time pressures.

    Social Behaviors Changing with Age: Observe how social behaviors change with age. This is a fascinating observation. Again a more efficient way to observe this is by watching TV shows that have characters of many ages (children, teens, young adults, older adults) and trying to observe subtle differences in their social demeanors.

    Compliments: Observe ways in which people tend to make others feel good; any time a person is making another feel good they are acting in a way that is complimentary. Notice that adults tend to act in a complimentary way rather than give overt verbal compliments. Notice your own social behaviors, and try to determine what you do that may be interpreted as being complimentary.

    Apologizing: Observe ways in which people tend to apologize. Notice that adults do not have to say they are sorry in order to show someone that they are sorry. While people may kick off their apology with words, often they follow with a set of complimentary actions that the other person interprets as showing remorse for their previous error that was worthy of an apology. Notice your own social behaviors and try and determine what you do to apologize. Do you start with saying you are sorry and follow through with subtle ways in which you show you are sorry by paying more positive attention to what a person is saying, etc?

Asking For Help: Observe how people you work or live with may ask for help. Try and determine if they are at their wits end when they ask for help, or quickly ask for help for something they may have been able to figure out or do themselves. You may observe that people are relatively quick to ask for help as it gives them the opportunity to engage with others and engage in some quick teamwork. How often do you ask for help? Do you tend to wait until you are desperate as you like to prove you can do everything yourself? Or do you have difficulty figuring out the timing of asking for help since you don't want to interrupt what others are doing? If you are not a person who asks for help, try to set a goal that you will ask someone in your work environment one time a day for help or just simply a clarifying question, such as "remind me, what time is our meeting today." Remember that asking for help is not simply to meet your needs but helps others to feel included and respected.

Greeting Others: Observe how people greet each other when they see each other in the morning and how the form of the greeting decreases in size as people run into each other across the day. For example, they may start with a verbal acknowledgement ("hi") while also looking in your direction and smiling; as the day progresses they may continue to acknowledge you by smiling but they don't expect you to literally say "hi" more than once a day! Now observe yourself, do you acknowledge people with greetings? If not, it is time to start to practice this by simply identifying one person in your office that you can greet each morning and then acknowledge with an exit greeting at the end of the day.

❖ The formula for greeting another person in the morning includes:

1. First establish eye contact prior to walking past the person.

2. As you walk past him or her, say 'Hi" or "How are you?" (especially if the person has returned the eye contact), all the while producing and maintaining a subtle smile.

3. Discontinue smiling as soon as you walk past them.

• Each week increase the number of people you greet, as your practice and confidence grow. Eventually you should be able to greet anyone who works in your place of business— this is expected. However, don't start with this large goal, or you will quickly become discouraged.

TIPS AND POINTERS BASED ON INFORMATION IN CHAPTER 3

- **Exploring emotions: Emotional Expression Compression**

    First and foremost, most of us use a physical strategy to try and release the internal pressure we are feeling such as taking three deep breaths, stretching or walking away from the situation that is causing immediate stress. Each of us has to find physical strategies to help calm us down to then allow us to think more clearly, developing a cognitive plan to help us navigate through difficult times. Determine what type of inner calming strategies you have found effective and cue yourself to use them.

    Some folks we work with have sensory issues, meaning their emotions tend to get increasingly flooded when exposed to certain sensory situations they find highly distracting or irritating. Some examples of situations that may trigger *sensory overload* can include but are not limited to incessant background noise, florescent lights, someone coming up and touching your shoulder or arm in the work environment or too many people talking to you at once. If sensory regulation issues appear to increase your emotional deregulation, and you have not found strategies to help calm your sensory system and related emotions, you may want to consult with an occupational therapist that specializes in sensory dysregulation. It is important to recognize that helping to establish a physical and sensory calm, even when upset, is key to organizing our mind with the more cerebral strategies described below.

Observe the difference in emotional reactions of children and adults. If you do not have much opportunity to observe children, try to watch episodes of a children's television show that has real children on it, such as *Sesame Street* or *Barney* (both on public broadcasting stations). Then observe television shows with solely adults on them, such as the evening news (where newscasters are to show minimal emotion), or shows that are part of a television series (medical shows, cops and robbers, situation comedies). Notice the difference between adults and children in the facial expressions used to convey similar emotions.

Watch a TV show with *the sound turned off* to observe how many emotions you can see if you focus on looking at the face—specifically from the cheekbones up through the forehead. People with social learning challenges tend to be overly dependent on the language used by characters, so by turning off the sound you tend to focus more on what is happening and observe more closely what people are feeling.

❖ Be aware the research shows that many persons with social learning challenges tend to focus their attention on the mouth, rather than the eyes, brow or cheeks. Observe what you look at when you look toward the face. If you do look at the mouth, push yourself to practice looking at what is called *the facial mask* (from the cheeks up to the brow) where most emotion is captured.

- ❖ If you want to watch more extreme emotions on the face, watch soap operas or movies where the characters are animated or made out of clay (claymation), such as *Toy Story* or *Wallace and Gromit*, but again watch with the sound turned off. The reason the emotions are more extreme in these genres is that the people who create them want to make you really feel the emotions; with the animated movies, making the facial mask more prominent convinces most of our brains that these animated characters are human.

- **Observing how we read or process emotional understanding**

  Watch the same TV shows described above, starting with shows for children, and observe how many different elements combine together to enable us to read emotions.

  - ❖ First start with the sound turned off and look at the different nonverbal cues, such as the face, the physical stance, hand or body gestures.

  - ❖ Turn the sound on and then listen for the verbal cues, such as the language spoken, the tone of voice, the volume of the voice.

  - ❖ If you observe an inconsistency between what someone says and how their facial expressions or body gestures, you may be observing sarcasm. See if you can identify acts of sarcasm versus pure acts of emotional honesty.

  - ❖ Observe how other people in a scene react once an emotion is conveyed. Watch for examples of emotional contagion. Then consider your own life and how you react based on how people respond to you emotionally.

- **Understanding how we share similar emotions for similar situations**

    Ask a family member, therapist or friend how they feel about specific events that they observe or experience or hear about that you know you have also reacted to emotionally.

    ❖ For example, if your supervisor corrects your work and implies you should do it a different way, you may feel frustrated or slightly saddened that you were not doing it correctly. Without telling a trusted adult how you felt about this experience, ask her how she feels, but first tell her to be totally honest with you. Let her know it is for your own investigation of how the social mind works. The tricky thing about talking about our emotions is that we are not used to talking about them honestly. Some people are simply not comfortable talking about their emotions and won't be completely honest even if you ask.

    ❖ Compare how this trusted person describes her emotional reaction in relation to yours. You should ask several people the same question so you can explore the range of reactions, then compare them to yours. While you may find that they don't exactly compare to your reaction, there is often a similar theme. What one person calls "frustrating" another person may describe as "annoying" or "maddening"; we do not have precise definitions for these words and how we use them, but they do establish a general tone of understanding.

- **Focusing on who we like and who we don't like**
  (Take time to stop and think about this.)

    Consider your own life experiences. Consider the qualities and characteristics of people you like. Can you observe a trend that these people tend to make you feel good about you? Now consider who you have not liked, why didn't you like them. Can you observe the trend that most people you don't like don't make you feel good about you?

- **Tracking your own and others' emotions on the Social Emotional Tracking Scale**
  (Go to page 35)

    Place your index finger on the center of the page, at the point where the "Fine" or "OK" line and the diagonal line converge. You can do this same activity using a pen to mark directly on the scale the subtle shifts in your emotions. If marking on the scale, make a photocopy of this page first so you can reuse it.

    Consider the last hour or two of your day at work or home; if that is too large a period then just begin now noticing your emotions every ten minutes or so. Shift your finger up or down the diagonal line, sliding it to each of the emotions you felt during that time period. Focus on the smaller feelings that made up each day—for example, annoyance that someone else was using the copier when you wanted it, satisfaction when you realized it was time to take your lunch break, boredom over a mundane work project or happiness at the end of the day when you got to go home but also irritation over the traffic you had to sit in.

    If you don't feel you are having any of the smaller, more subtle emotions, but find that you only have large emotions such as anger or elation, your focus will be on learning to identify and respond in more subtle ways to the world around you. Talk to your therapist about this.

    Now consider how you may have expressed your emotions, if at all. Would others around you have known how you were feeling at each moment? Would they have described you as having a larger or smaller emotional response than the one you reported for each situation? (Some people have very large responses compared with what they describe as mild emotions, or vice versa.)

Think about how each one of your emotions, or a lack of emotion, may have altered the way you responded to a person or situation.

Try this exercise on different days or at different time periods in the day to better understand and narrow the focus on your emotional navigation system. Before we can improve our social skills, we have to understand our emotions better since the only reason we all use social skills is to impact other's emotions! *Being polite* can be translated to mean acting in a way that makes others feel good about themselves.

- **Using the Problem-Solving Thermometer**
  (Go to page 41)

    Remember: What someone calls a size one problem and another call a size two problem may be subjective, but what one person calls a size one problem is likely not a size ten problem to another person, if both experienced the same problem. As with our emotions, we are expected to recognize and respond to problems in similar ways across many people.

    Consider some of the problems you have encountered at work or home, and then place them on the Problem-solving Thermometer. A devastating hurricane or earthquake that destroys your house would be a size ten problem, while dropping a file on the floor at work is a size one problem. The size of a problem also depends on the context. Misplacing a legal contract may feel like a size three or four problem, but it becomes much bigger if you get called in by your supervisor to discuss your weak organizational skills.

❖ Show your chart to trusted friends, family or counselors. See if they would agree with the way you have classified the size of your problem. If they disagree, ask them to explain how they perceive the size of the problem. As with emotions, it is not expected that your number system will match exactly with theirs, but if you think a problem is a size seven, and they think it is a size three problem, this may indicate that you are perceived as overreacting to the problems you encounter on a daily basis.

Now consider your emotional response as observed by others, based on the problem you perceive you are having. Is it in line with what others expect? Ask your trusted advisor. For example:

❖ A size one problem like the dropped file should result in a size one emotion, such as muttering "darn" under our breath.

❖ A size seven problem could cause us to feel anxiety, sadness and frustration or embarrassment, but we would still be careful about revealing these emotions (remember emotional expression compression). When this level of problem is handled well, people who are experiencing the stress of a size seven or eight problem can stay calm and continue to relate to those around them so they don't burn any bridges. If you upset others based on how you react to your own problem, it will be difficult to have people help you with your problem-solving process; in fact you may have just created more problems for yourself.

❖ On the rare occasion when we actually have a size ten problem, an all-out display of emotion or grief is permissible, as long as people are aware of the situation. Most size ten problems happen outside of the work environment (for example, death or destruction), and it is understood that people need to leave work (perhaps take a leave of absence) to deal with this level of emotional and physical stress or devastation.

Practice labeling the size of your problem and then observing your emotional reaction to see if it is aligned with how other people react and respond to a similar-sized problem. Some people have difficulty coping with small problems and unintentionally make them appear much bigger with an oversized emotional reaction. Learning to see your problems on a scale, and working to control the degree of your emotional responses as they relate to the different-sized problems, can help in many ways. Not only are your emotional reactions more in step with what coworkers would expect, but taming the emotional response also allows you to think more clearly. Ultimately, the more you participate in your problem-solving and emotional response process, the more you will be perceived as a steady person whom others can depend on.

- **Better understanding of how we read each other's emotions and intentions**

    Observe that you try to figure out what people are doing, where they are going or why they are doing what they are doing. We don't do this with every single person who is near us, but we should be generally aware of what people are doing when they are close to us.

    Recognize that other people have these very same thoughts about you. Even when you don't intend to communicate, your mere existence in an environment you share with others makes people aware of your presence as well as their own consideration of your motives and intentions—verbal and nonverbal. *This is critical to consider in order to understand how people are reading you—your actions and the meaning of your language—even if you did not intend to literally communicate with them.*

- ❖ A tip for those who tend to talk to themselves: People who talk to themselves generate uncomfortable thoughts in others. The social rule with regards to language use is that spoken language is intention driven; hence people expect that when you talk, you are talking to someone. If you are talking to yourself, people then may then have weird thoughts about you since they don't think you are using language the way it was intended. If you have a strong need to talk to yourself, put on a set of telephone earphones; now people will simply think you are talking on the phone.

- **Beginning to explore how people interpret your responses to their thoughts and emotions**

  Observe how you are responding to others' thoughts and emotions.

  - ❖ It is expected that you are in sync with how others feel. If they are showing that they feel sad about something, is your face matching their expression? If you feel you are weak at this, work with a counselor to practice having her tell you incidents from her life, good and bad, and then match your facial expression subtly to what she is saying. Videotape yourself and watch the face of your counselor as well as your own reaction. It takes practice to do this well; allow that you may look awkward practicing this at first but this is the practice you need.

TIPS AND POINTERS BASED ON INFORMATION IN CHAPTER 4

- **Exploring other areas of perspective-taking.**

  Exploring your own and others' thoughts, emotions and intentions has already been introduced in the tips and pointers above. We will briefly explore further the following concepts related to perspective-taking:

Belief Systems: Consider your own belief systems and how you came to own them. You will find that many of them were either introduced to you as part of your family's values or through forming your own opinions as you grew up. Beliefs are opinions, and an opinion is just one point of view.

❖ Challenging another's belief system can cause the person you are challenging to feel strong negative emotions towards you as the challenger. To **respect** someone's belief system is usually to know they have a different belief than you and to ignore the topic all together.

❖ Asking too many questions about why someone believes what they do is considered a challenge, since the person to whom the questions are directed may interpret that your motive is to challenge their entire belief system.

❖ It is fine to openly discuss belief systems in a situation where you know (or you think you know) that everyone shares the same belief system. In a place of religious worship, you can talk about your faith. On the job the workforce is typically multicultural, with many and varied belief systems. In this environment it is best to ignore the differences you notice in others (faith, skin color) and focus on your common traits— for example, the jobs you do for the business that employs you or your family life.

Prior knowledge and Experience: Observe how adults use language. Notice they don't talk in tremendous detail; instead they tend to talk in concepts. When asked, "What did you do for lunch?" they usually don't start by discussing the mode of transportation used to go eat lunch, nor do they say specifically what they ate. Instead they simply tell you where they went, "I went to an Italian place" or in general what they had, "I grabbed a burger." Notice that people tend to be aware of what another person already knows about the topic being discussed, and they only share a main idea related to what they think their conversational partner doesn't know.

- ❖ Explore how you use language to answer others' questions or to explain what you are doing. Are you a person who people think overexplains an answer?

- ❖ While talking to others, catch yourself thinking about what the other person knows or doesn't know about a topic before you provide your own answer to their question. If your brain does not tend to do this, and you tend to assume people do not know what you are talking about since they are not exactly you, you will likely need to work with an advisor to figure out what you can assume people know or don't know as they create their lessons.

As you work with advisors, be patient. While many of us adapt our language by considering other people's prior knowledge and shared experiences about the world, few of us realize we are doing this. Thus this will be a new experience for them to think about as well.

TIPS AND POINTERS BASED ON INFORMATION IN CHAPTER 5

- **Here is a brief exploration of the Four Steps of Communication**

    Step 1: Think about what you know about people you want or need to communicate with.

    - ❖ Observe how your own mind stores information about people you have met before. The more familiar you are with a person, the more you remember about them.

- ❖ Recognize that you are to think about what you may already know about a person when you plan to speak to him or her. This practice helps you to recognize what the person already knows or what they know about you, which can help you be more concise with your language-based explanations. This practice also guides you to know how to direct your comments and questions to a person. When you talk to a person that you have some familiarity with and show them what you remember about them, you are indirectly complimenting them by sending a message that they are important enough for you to have put this information into your memory.

- ❖ If you do not know the person you are about to speak to, recognize what you can infer about this person by the mere fact they are in the same place as you at the same time. For example, if you are both employed by the same company, you can talk to them about their job or how long they have worked there. There is always a way to find a shared experience that you can consider for possible discussion once you realize what you may have in common—even if you have never met before. (For example, if the two of you are in a store, you have in common that you are looking at the same merchandise; if you are in a line at the Department of Motor Vehicles, you likely share the same frustration with waiting in the line, and so on.)

- ❖ At this step of communication you are not actually talking to the person; you are just learning to appreciate that each of us spends a brief amount of time getting our thoughts organized about who we are with prior to our speaking to them.

Step 2: Study your physical presence and that of others. Start by observing how people move in space to show their

Good Intentions Are Not Good Enough

intent to communicate with others or to demonstrate their desire to avoid communication.

- ❖ Observe the subtle and fairly slow way by which people approach each other. Notice the subtle shifts in people's postures, hips, stance and head to show they are approaching another person with the desire to communicate.

- ❖ Pay special attention to what people do with their arms when they are standing in the presence of others.

- ❖ Persons who use minimal hand gestures when talking tend to let their arms hang at their sides. This is generally perceived as an awkward or odd stance. Explore different things you can do with your arms while talking to avoid letting them hang at your side.

- ❖ Observe the distance at which people stand from each other while communicating. Can you see when people are standing too close or too far apart?

- ❖ Observe your own physical approach and notice where you are standing. Think about how another person perceives your physical presence. If you have the chance to work with an advisor, have them videotape your movement while you approach a person and stand and show interest in that person. Note how you shift away from that person when you are done talking to them.

- ❖ Advisors and clients tend to not want to practice or explore the role of body positioning in communication. People often feel that it is overly simplistic or condescending to observe and practice something that is thought to be such a common practice. Don't give in to that point of view. Many of our clients struggle tremendously with subtle shifts in the body, posture and positioning of their arms when standing in the presence of others. This area of behavior requires observation, exploration and practice. Don't combine this step with conversation. The way to become more familiar with this area is to study different aspects of the communication process in isolation before combining them together again.

Step 3: Think with your eyes: Read this section in the book carefully. Consider how you use your eyes not only to act like you are listening to others but also to study the face, postures and context in which you are communicating with the other person. Watch the eye gaze of your communication partner to infer what he or she is thinking about as well.

- ❖ Explain to a trusted advisor the difference between merely making eye contact with another versus what you learn about people when you *think with your eyes*.

- ❖ Observe how people show whom they are talking to by whom they are looking at. If someone looks at you and asks you a question, this means they are likely talking to you, even if they have not specifically used your name.

- ❖ Observe people you don't know looking at things in a store, in the community and so on. See if you can infer what people are thinking about based on where they are looking. This is important! Don't skip this step. Too often my clients have said they are not comfortable looking at others, so they simply don't. But in choosing that option, they miss out on a lot of important information they are not interpreting about those around them.

- ❖ If you have a sensory aversion to looking at people in the eye, realize that most of us do not stare at the eyes of others when we are talking to them. We are all adverse to the idea that someone would simply stare at our eyes. Instead, explore the part of the facial mask (cheek bones through the brow) that you are comfortable looking at.

- ❖ Practice looking at parts of a trusted advisor's face, and have him tell you where he thinks you are looking. What you will likely find is that if you are looking at a point within an inch from his eyes, he will often think you are looking at his eyes.

- ❖ Sit in a small room with this same advisor. Have him look at an object on the wall or in some other location of the room, but don't have him tell you what he is looking at. Try this with many different objects many different times. See if you are good at inferring what your advisor is looking at by reading the direction his eyes are gazing. If he confirms you are correct, this is a good start to building your confidence in using your ability to think with your eyes. However, not everyone has mastered this skill, even if they have advanced degrees from universities. If you are weak at this skill, it is important to practice getting better at making this inference.

- ❖ Once you have inferred accurately what your advisor is looking at, now have him look a singular object in the room again, and this time tell him what you think he is thinking about. Try this with many different objects many different times. Watch your brain move from looking at an object to thinking about a concept. For example, if your advisor is *looking* at a clock you need to say he is *thinking* about the time. See if you can reliably predict what someone is thinking about, and if not, keep practicing.

- ❖ Explore how you track what people are thinking about while in less structured situations, such as during your conversations with them.

Step 4: Use language to relate to others by practicing different types of comments and questions.

- ❖ Review the definitions of different types of questions used to communicate in this chapter. The two key questions are those we use to ask people for more information about themselves versus baiting questions, which we ask people to get them to focus on what we want to talk about.

- ❖ Begin by simply observing people talk to each in a social conversation. Notice how they shift from asking questions to inquire about others to providing supporting comments to adding their own thoughts. Try to differentiate these language functions in your own mind by studying them and seeing how people combine these different techniques into what we consider to a conversation.

- ❖ Practice different elements of the conversation by focusing on one element at a time. Once again, clients and their advisors tend to fail to appreciate the complexity of how people appear to make this look so simple. The job of the person with a social learning weakness—with the help of a trusted advisor—is to figure out which of these elements the person is already good at using and which need more practice. When it comes to practicing them, do not practice them all at once; instead practice each of the weaker skills in isolation. You can only learn to improve if you can study something in its more basic state. From this author's perspective, a mistake that is often made when helping folks with social learning challenges is that advisors tend to just tell them to practice conversing. But how do they know what to practice if they don't know what elements or tools are used to create conversational language?

4. Asking questions of people about those people

   a. Consider the first step of communication—thinking about what you know about the person you are talking to. Then consider what it is you don't know about them that is related to this information, and ask them a question about that. Realize that we do this in part to show an interest in the other person while letting them know what we remember about them; this is a hidden compliment. It is also expected that we wonder how people are, what they have been doing and what is new in their lives. We are supposed to show signs of social curiosity without prying too deeply into what is considered personal information.

      i. It is safe to ask people about topic such as their families, their jobs, plans for vacation, hobbies, preferred books, TV shows or movies.

      ii. It is not safe to ask a person how she or he is doing with regards to his or her sex life, dating history, marriage or problems you may have remembered the person has experienced in the past that may be the cause of embarrassment if you bring them up. In our culture, we are also not supposed to ask women how old they are, but it is fine to ask this question of children and most men. This is one of those weird hidden rules.

   b. While this sounds simple to do once it is explained, again it is a skill that should only be considered easy for those who have practiced doing it since they were children. If you are working with an advisor, literally practice trying to recall what you remember about someone and then figuring out what you don't know and formulating a question.

5. Baiting questions: I have found that most of my clients are good at asking baiting questions. However, I want people to study and know the difference between a question they ask to show genuine interest in another person and a question asked to lure someone into the questioner's web of desired conversational topics.

6. Supportive comments: Use small comments (verbal and nonverbal) to show you are listening or to show you understand another's experience; this is considered a mandatory and a positive thing to do.

    a. Observe your own communication style. How good are you at giving feedback by nodding your head in agreement to show you are listening while making little comments like, "Oh," "Huh," and so on. Also explore how you provide supportive statement such as "That sounds nice" or "That could not have been fun."

    b. If you or your advisor believes you don't actively provide feedback or offer supportive statements, then simply practice this one element of communication. Focus on it as you practice giving little supporting comments or gestures to your conversational partner. As odd as this may feel, do not actually have a full conversation. Your advisor is to talk and tell you about different experiences, and your job is to simply practice these supporting comments. I have worked with many adults who do not provide this type of subtle but important feedback. If you fail to do this, then people may think you are not an active listener.

7. Adding your own thoughts: Monitor how well you are able to comment and share how your experiences link to something someone else said in a social conversation. Some of my clients do this extremely well (these are the ones who usually have to practice asking more questions of others), while other clients feel completely unskilled in figuring out how to connect their own experiences to others. For those who have difficulty with this step, try the following:

   a. Listen to what people have to say about their own lives. People actually spend a lot of time talking about themselves.

   b. Imagine their experiences based on your own experiences of the world. For example, if they are talking about going on a trip to Hawaii, even if you never have been there, imagine what you know about Hawaii based on knowledge you have gained in your life.

   c. Add a thought from your own experience as it connects or fails to connect to theirs. For example, if you have never been to Hawaii, or in fact you have really spent little time near any ocean, you can add your own thought by saying, "I have never spent much time near an ocean, but I do love to go on vacation. Last year I enjoyed just staying home and watching some old movies; one of them showed Hawaii. It looked beautiful!" If you have been to the ocean, you can say, "That sounds great, I love going to the ocean. Last time I went we were in San Francisco—that's a beautiful city." In both of these examples, the person who is adding their thought is shifting the conversation to their own experience while still connecting what they are talking about to what their conversational partner had mentioned.

d. Practice adding your thoughts to the thoughts of others. Observe how you are not actually maintaining the conversation. Instead you are maintaining a connection to what some else said. Over the course of a conversation grounded in add-a-thought comments, you will find that the actual topic is difficult to define, but in retrospect you can show how the conversation moved from one discussion point to another.

8. Whopping Topic Changes: Simply stated, whopping topic changes (WTCs) occur when someone makes a comment, and no one can figure out how it linked back to previous comments. For example, a person might say, "I can't wait for the weekend," and someone else may respond, "I hate fancy restaurant.," In this case people may have a weird thought about this response since it fails to show a link to the previous statement and appeared to be a WTC. However, if the person who responded were to explain further to say, "This weekend I am supposed to go to a fancy restaurant, and I hate having to dress up and pay all the extra money," you would have no problem with the comment. We need to narrate our responses so people can see the obvious connection between how their statement made you think and then respond about your own life.

9. Merging the concepts together: As you get better at practicing these concepts in isolation and feel you have increased your proficiency with regard to your weaker skills, now begin to use the different concepts in combination. Practice asking people questions about them, listen to their response and

then add your own thought. However, don't expect that you should be able to do this in a period of days or weeks. It often takes months of practice to feel anything close to a basic level of familiarity with these concepts that you have not practiced previously. To avoid being discouraged, track your progress one small step at a time.

10. Conversational expectations if you are married or in an intimate relationship:

   a. It is expected that you wonder how your partner's day was if you were not with her or him during the day. Simply asking, "How was your day" or "What did you do today" can go a long way toward showing another person you are interested in their lives. Too many spouses or partners don't ask this type of question, thinking that if the spouse had something special to share about their day they would simply say it. Remember, conversations are not about logic, they are more about showing others you are interested in them! If you ask how their day was, it is implied that you care about them.

   b. It is also expected that while you may spend a lot of time together and share many of the same experiences, what you will never fully know is how that person felt about the experience. Asking, "Did you like that?" or "What did you think about the dinner?" shows that you are interested in your spouse's or partner's opinion and feelings as distinct from your own.

   c. Remember to take the time to thank your partner for anything he or she did to make your life more comfortable. For example, if he made you dinner, say "Thank you for dinner, it was very good!" Showing your partner you are considering how she spent her time to help you, and letting her know she made you feel good, makes her feel good in return.

11. Conversational expectations when you work closely with other people across the workday: Those who work closely with others while at work may do some of the same things recommended in the previous steps. When you stop to think about it, at times we spend as much time talking to our colleagues as we do our partners or spouses. Letting your coworkers know you appreciate them once in a while—by asking about their lives, providing supportive comments, adding your own thoughts to supplement their experiences and even letting them know that they are helpful to you—can go a long way toward building team work.

TIPS AND POINTERS BASED ON INFORMATION IN CHAPTER 6

- **Getting to the core of communication. Observing how we adjust our communication in different situations.**

    Pay close attention to how people use the four steps of communication a bit differently in different situations.

    ❖ Observe the differences in communication style in the following situations:

    1. A formal meeting
    2. A casual meeting
    3. A one-on-one, work-based conversation
    4. A social conversation in the work setting

5. A social conversation outside of the work setting

❖ Observe how our physical presence may be stiffer or more formal in some of these situations and far more relaxed in others.

❖ Observe how the use of language shifts during different situations; some settings allow for far more casual use of language, including the possible use of swear words, while other settings dictate only more polite language is to be used.

❖ Observe how people who know each other well only talk about specific work-related topics in some settings, and talk about topics related to their personal lives in other settings.

❖ Observe how and when you adapt your own behaviors to correlate with the hidden rules of formality or lack of formality dictated by each of these settings.

❖ If you tend to always respond with one set of behaviors regardless of settings, practice adjusting different aspects of how you present yourself in different settings. For example, if you tend to be formal and stiff with your body, practice sitting in more relaxed postures in what you observe to be more relaxed settings. Again, while I can make this sound simple, it is not easy to match the subtle differences in formality dictated by the difference situations for a person who has no familiarity with shifting subtle behaviors of the body, language use and so on. To encourage patience for all involved in this learning process, the best thing for an advisor to do is to imagine how difficult all these skills would be to learn if your brain had not pushed you to learn them intuitively.

- **Appreciating the genuine importance of the social fake and practicing faking it!**

    The social fake is genuinely important in social interactions, even though that comment may sounds disingenuous! Showing people you are interested in what they are saying or doing when you are actually not all that fascinated can keep people connected to each other through our boring moments. The truth is that at a very basic level, even people we love dearly do not always interest us highly by what they say or do. To tell them or actively imply to them they are boring us is considered highly insulting. While you do not want to spend your life faking all reactions and interest in others, there are times when it is beneficial to do this. It would be nearly impossible to keep any friend or family member wanting to relate to you if you did not fake your interest in what they are talking about or showing you at least some of the time. As I have repeated many times during the course of this book, how you make people feel is more important than actually telling them the truth all of the time.

    Re-read the story about Carl in this chapter if you find the concept of the social fake unpalatable. Then observe how you expect others to treat you to keep you feeling good about the way they interact with you. Observe ways in which you can mirror those types of social behaviors as you provide a sense that you are also an active listener and a supportive conversational partner.

- **Indirect language: Continue to expose yourself to the fact that much of meaning we communicate is carried by what is not spoken aloud**

    Review the section on this in the chapter. Go over the various statements and the ways people perceive their meaning. Recognize that interpreting language-based meanings is one of the most complicated things the brain does!

    Explore your own belief system when it comes to the use of

language. I have had clients insist that they only say exactly what they mean and are exasperated when people perceive their message differently than they had intended. Explore what it means to *perceive, intuit* or *infer* meaning, rather than to assume automatically that everyone will understand you exactly as you expect to be understood.

Recognize in yourself that you make judgments about what you think people meant by what they said. Anything you do means that others will do it as well.

Practice thinking and interpreting language in more flexible ways. Read the cartoons or sarcastic greeting cards that are displayed in many pharmacies or gift stores to try and discern how we play with the meaning of words. Try to interpret how the cartoonists or writers use words to convey different types of meaning, often with hilarious outcomes. *The Far Side®,* a set of cartoons created by Gary Larson, often takes our language and twists the meaning into new and fun ways so that words and phrases are perceived differently.

Explore how we use language to convey different types of meaning in our conversations, without meaning to be funny but to express ourselves more creatively or efficiently.

Continue to explore what we mean when we say language is an inference; you have to read between the lines to determine what was meant by what was said. One tip in understanding this is that you are not only to focus on what was stated aloud, but also how the message was stated given the various other elements communicated (tone of voice, facial expression).

Most importantly, consider what you think the speaker's intended message was as you try and interpret what other persons are saying. For example, when watching a commercial on TV we know the intent is to encourage you to consider buying the product being advertised. Knowing this, shapes how you interpret what they are telling you. Then watch an infomercial (the thirty-minute paid-for advertisements often shown on more obscure channels or on popular channels during times when fewer people watch TV). Listen to the language. Most people know that much of what is said on an infomercial is bending the truth to the point of lying; therefore we often don't take seriously what they are saying or even demonstrating for us as they try and pitch their product. While you consider how advertisements have a clear intention, recognize that all language is intention driven. When you think about why someone may be telling you something, learn to get better at considering what they really mean by what they say, and then judge for yourself whether you think they are being truthful or insincere.

Try to perceive how people read your intentions. People are trying to interpret what you mean by what you say, just like you are trying to perceive what they mean by what they say.

Assess yourself to see if you tend to be literal-minded. If you know that your brain does not do this well, do not insist you understood what people meant by what you heard them say. This could lead to you being seen as a contentious person.

Appreciate that the ideas presented here are simply to get you thinking and are only the tip of the iceberg in understanding how we process and practice better understanding of what we refer to as *abstract language*.

TIPS AND POINTERS BASED ON INFORMATION IN CHAPTER 7

- **Conformity, networking and teamwork**

    If you have a visceral reaction to the concepts of conformity, networking and teamwork, remember that no one is encouraging you to not be recognized for the unique individual that you are. It is more about the fact that people as a whole struggle to recognize the positive attributes of those around them if they don't feel those people are contributing in a positive way to others' well being. Each person on earth tends to be pretty egocentric; we need to help people to feel we value them as part of the formula for them valuing us. As people value us (in part for showing our care and interest in them), then they validate us. As humans we have a strong emotional need to be validated by others, whether we recognize this or not. This goes for all persons, including those born to weaker social communication skills. Just because your brain did not make this as easy for you to do, it does not mean you don't seek others to appreciate your place on this earth. The strategies embedded in this chapter may help you to see how you can work on this for yourself, depending on your own emerging awareness of your social strengths that you can celebrate and weaknesses you have identified to work on.

As also mentioned throughout this book, there are few people who walk among us who don't think they have to continue to work at bettering their social skills, even if they were born to what is perceived as a normal or neurotypical social intelligence.

TIPS AND POINTERS BASED ON INFORMATION IN CHAPTER 8

- **From friendly to friendship—recognizing and working on different levels of friendship**

    The idea that we all have a ton of friends is marketed heavily by social networking sites such as Facebook or Linkedin. The reality is that many adults have a relatively small circle of friends and that there is a significant difference between being friendly and a real friendship.

As seamlessly as many people appear to make and keep friends, what people don't generally talk about is the fact they actually work at sustaining their friendships. Friendships require organizational skills; you have to remember to contact your friends and arrange times to meet with them to rekindle social connections, especially if you have not seen them for awhile. E-mailing, texting and IMing (instant messaging) helps in that these tools provide very quick ways to let someone know you are thinking about them without needing to put aside a significant amount of time to communicate.

The following hierarchy is an attempt to show how we evolve from greeting a person to having a friend.

- ❖ Level 1. Greetings: You extend greetings to people by whom you want to be perceived as friendly, but you really don't know them or don't talk to them on a regular basis. You should greet many more people than you are actually friends with. Being perceived as friendly does not mean you have friends, but it is a first step.

- ❖ Level 2. Acquaintances: You've had some small discussions with these persons, usually because you work with them or they are friends of a friend, so you happened to hang out with them for a short while. However, you do not go out of your way to seek them out.

- ❖ Level 3. Developing work-based friendships: You're already acquaintances, and you both think you'd like to talk to each other more often. At work you might ask that person what they are doing for lunch and arrange to eat with him or her, or you might stop by their desk to say "Hi" and quickly touch base with them. If you are interested in developing a friendship with them that extends beyond work, you may "friend" them on Facebook them or connect with them on some other form of social networking site or shared-interest chat room.

- ❖ Level 4. Bonded friends: This is the type of friendship where people are "there for each other" beyond just having a work-based friendship. You go out of your way to connect with this person outside of the work environment, and when together you do not only talk about work.

- ❖ Level 5. Very close friend: With a very close friend it is expected you do all the things mentioned in the previous levels, but with a bit more intensity. It is expected that you have deeper conversations about both pleasant and distressing topics with this person when either of you need to. This is the person you can really open up to. Not everyone has a really close friend, and most people only have one or two at any time. Few people have a lot (five or more) of very close friends.

- ❖ Understanding the transient nature of friendship: On again-off again friends. Over the course of your life people will come and go based on how you met them, where they or you are in your own stage of life, and so on. If you meet people at your job and become bonded friends with them, this does not mean you are friends for life; it means that at this point in your life they are very important to you. However, if you change jobs and don't get to see these people on a regular basis, you may not maintain as intense a friendship; in fact you may rarely talk to them even though you once spent a lot of time with them. The fact that you have not spoken to them for a year or even five years does not mean you dislike the person, it just means life got in the way. You still have memories of the person, and when and if you meet again, you may find that you strike up a great conversation and once again enjoy each other's company even if you just see them for one night every few years. For most people the majority of their friendships are *on again-off again friendships*; these are real friendships that are to be valued in many ways, including using these friends to network with about job openings they may be aware of when you are looking for a new job.

Now how to learn to move from one level to the next along the path of developing more friendships.

- ❖ Think of one or two people you'd like to be better, more personal friends with and get to know more. These may be peers you notice because they seem to be nice, you like how they handle themselves, you like their sense of humor and they seem to see you as a person who they also think is friendly. Consider whether they also seem to enjoy your company. When you have been friendly to them in the past did they respond in kind? If so, this may be a person who welcomes your friendship as well; there is an implied agreement made consisting of nonverbal cues between two people that shows they both want to become friends that precedes genuine friendship. The nonverbal cues are those that demonstrate to each other that you both enjoy each other's company. These cues consist of many aspects already described in the previous tips and pointers. If a person seems to reject being friendly with you, turn your friendly attention elsewhere. No one likes to be repeatedly rejected by someone, and not all people are designed to be friends with each other.

- ❖ Look at the sequence of friendship and identify to see what level of friendship you currently have with people you know. Are they "Friendly", an "Acquaintance", or maybe even a "Developing Friendship"? Whatever level you are at with a person is where you begin to work purposefully toward advancing a friendship. If you have seen a person at the office who you perceive as being nice, but you have never even greeted him or her, then start with a greeting. If they return your greeting, you may want to start asking them how their day is going, and now you are moving towards becoming an acquaintance or perhaps eventually a friend.

❖ Look at the ideas listed above and choose one or two things you can do differently to move along toward friendship—meaning to help that person notice you want to become a better friend. For example, if you have an acquaintance and you want to actively develop a friendship, ask that person to meet you for a cup of coffee or perhaps lunch.

❖ Continue to monitor the nonverbal cues of the person you are being increasingly friendly with. If he or she responds positively to you and in fact may reciprocate gestures of friendship, continue in this direction. If they repeatedly have reasons for not wanting to get together with you, consider this a subtle way of letting you know they don't want to pursue the friendship; and visa versa, if you don't want to continue in the friendship trajectory, then make excuses for why you can't meet up them. Adults do not usually tell other adults, "I don't want to be friends with you"; they would only do this if they perceive someone is overbearing in their outreach to be friends, and they are not reading the more subtle cues of rejection.

❖ How long does it take to make a bonded friend? This depends on the people and the situation. There are times when people move from being friendly to develop an intense friendship within a day or two of meeting. Other friendships lag and stall at the level of acquaintance and can remain that way for years before moving up toward a developing or bonded friend.

These stages of progressing in friendship are not marked by time but instead by the quality of the relationship. True bonded and close friends are people we can really trust, and it takes time to develop a strong sense of trust in another person.

How does any social anxiety add to the complication of evolving friendships?

❖ Social anxiety can prevent you from accessing the social information you know to be true and the social skills you may have intact. Social anxiety can also shut you down from practicing all of the concepts and skills reviewed in this book, thus those with strong social anxiety may have less developed social skills as they simply have lacked practice.

❖ Unfortunately, social anxiety appears to be strongly correlated with having weaker development of social thinking and related social skills. However, it is possible to be born anxious but with capable social skills. But the years of ceding to the anxiety may have provided less practice, making you feel you are less capable by the time you are an adult.

❖ You can help yourself overcome social anxiety by reminding yourself that you understand the concepts behind social thinking and that you have reasonably competent social skills. Then you have to encourage yourself, step by step, to seek the practice needed to prove to yourself you are able to socialize without people having uncomfortable thoughts about you. I posted the following piece of writing on my Web site about the work we have done at our clinic to help people through the process of coping with their related social anxiety.

AN IMPORTANT NOTE
What about those who may truly have social anxiety and already have many social competencies?

"Based on our growing experience, it appears that some of our students have far more anxiety than they do lack of social knowledge and related ability. For these students, we still find that helping them through their anxiety has a lot to do with helping them explore and practice their social competencies. The Social Thinking teachings helped to put this all into context. Thus, these same lessons have shown to be helpful to them as well.

It is always a good idea to have a mental health professional on your team to help with all of this, but our mental health professionals (counselors/social workers/psychologists, etc.) will do well to become familiar with how to teach Social Thinking and related social competencies/skills.

A book for high-level teens and young adults to read to help them learn about the intricacies of the social mind and how to learn new social competencies is entitled *Socially Curious and Curiously Social: A Social Thinking Guidebook for Bright Teens and Young Adults* (Winner and Crooke, 2009). However, we have also learned from many professionals that this book was helpful for them to read, as it teaches directly how we address various topics with our older kids, young adults and in fact our adult population. As Pam and I completed writing this book, we decided not to put in a chapter on anxiety since the book was already longer than we had hoped (we added the chapter on the difference between being friendly and making friends in the 11th hour!), so the above summarizes what we would have written. I have yet to put this in a publication but thought I would share it here since many have found it very helpful (including our adult clients!)." — *Michelle and Pam*

TIPS AND POINTERS BASED ON INFORMATION IN CHAPTER 9

- **Social Technology and Social Thinking**

    One of the strengths of social technology is that it allows a much easier way to communicate with others and acquire a sense of validation. Communication via e-mail, chats, IMing remove some of the many demands that feel overwhelming to folks with social learning challenges. Not having to process and respond to the tone of voice, eye contact or physical cues while also having a longer period of time for the response to be developed makes electronic communication much more comfortable and inviting to those who struggle to multitask socially. All that being said, nothing quite replace the face-to-face validation of interpersonal contact. Having someone to meet at a restaurant or go out into the community with feels good.

    If you are a person who finds much more comfort in electronic forms of communication, continue to use this as a means to relax and respond to others in a way that meets many of your social needs. However, continue to push yourself to learn more about relating to others face to face. For some people online relationships can be addicting, making it increasingly difficult to leave their computer to continue to do the projects that allow them to keep their job or venture out into their community to grocery shop, relate to others in their neighborhood or even take the time to take care of their basic hygiene. Everything is good in moderation, including taking the time to continue to work on improving one's social competencies.

TIPS AND POINTERS BASED ON INFORMATION IN CHAPTER 10

- **Practicing the use of Social Behavior Mapping**

    Employ the template and description reviewed in this chapter to use a Social Behavior Map for adults (pages 162-167).

    ❖ Photocopy the map.

    ❖ Explore a concrete situation in which you have experienced some specific challenges. It may be very helpful to have an advisor (family member, counselor, teacher, trusted friend) review this with you.

    ❖ Remember, don't shoot the messenger! We did not create these rules; we are simply trying to help you to engage more effectively in the experience of the social mind to help you be better responded to in your community.

    ❖ Fold the map so that you only see the first and last columns on the expected or unexpected side. Notice that when you do this, you will observe that when each of us does the unexpected, we end up feeling worse about ourselves! When we do the expected, we end up feeling better about ourselves. This means that ultimately we serve ourselves better if we do what is expected.

We continue to develop new ideas for helping adults to explore more advanced ways of learning about the social mind; you will find up-to-date announcements and postings of new ideas on our website, www.socialthinking.com.

SocialThinking has so much to offer!

OUR MISSION

At Social Thinking, our mission is to help people develop their social competencies to better connect with others and experience deeper well being. We create unique treatment frameworks and strategies to help individuals develop their social thinking and related skills to meet their academic, personal, and professional social goals. These goals often included sharing space effectively with others, learning to work as part of a team, and developing relationships of all kinds: with family, friends, classmates, co-workers, romantic partners, etc.

ARTICLES
100+ free educational articles and treatment strategies

LIVESTREAM EVENTS, ON DEMAND COURSES & CUSTOM TRAINING
Live and recorded trainings for schools and organizations

PRODUCTS
Books, games, posters, music and more!

CLINICAL RESEARCH
Measuring the effectiveness of the Social Thinking Methodology

TREATMENT: CHILDREN & ADULTS
Clinical treatment, assessments, school consultations, etc.

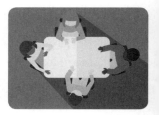

CLINICAL TRAINING PROGRAM
Three-day intensive training for professionals

www.socialthinking.com